Ox Cart to Automobile

Social Change
in Western New York

Thomas Rasmussen

To Jack and Therese,

Do you think this story about
social change in western New York
is relevant in rural Georgia on this
side of the Appalachians?

Tom Rasmussen

UNIVERSITY PRESS OF AMERICA,® INC.
Lanham • Boulder • New York • Toronto • Plymouth, UK

Copyright © 2009 by
University Press of America,® Inc.
4501 Forbes Boulevard
Suite 200
Lanham, Maryland 20706
UPA Acquisitions Department (301) 459-3366

Estover Road
Plymouth PL6 7PY
United Kingdom

Library of Congress Control Number: 2009925761
ISBN: 978-0-7618-4588-1 (paperback : alk. paper)
eISBN: 978-0-7618-4589-8

For the People of Allegany County

Past and Present

Contents

Preface   vii

1   Organizing Ideas: Central Place and Prisoner's Dilemma   1
     The Importance of Transportation Costs   1
     Specialization and Economies of Scale   3
     Politics and Game Theory   5
     Why Focus on One Western New York County?   10

2   Distance, Elevation and Early Settlement Decisions   13
     The Legacy of Rocks and Ice   13
     Where Did Early Migrants Choose To Settle?   15
     Friends, Neighbors, and Early Settlement   19
     Early Farms and Distance from Commercial Centers   20
     Elevation and Early Settlement   22
     Local Villages as Central Places   28
     Road Building in Allegany County   30

3   Making Farms and Raising Crops 1810–1850   34
     The Collapse of Iroquois Power in Western New York   34
     Creditors and Debtors: Land Speculators and Early Settlers   37
     Carving a Farm in the Wilderness   44
     Standard of Living in the Frontier Cabin   50
     Beginnings of the Dairy Industry   52
     Conflict and Cooperation: Games among Neighbors   53
     Politics: Local Factions, Whigs and Democrats   58
     Taming Nature and Building Home   62

4   The Western New York Farm at Mid-Century   68
    Transition from Subsistence to Cash Crop Farming   68
    The Village as Commercial Center   74
    A Snapshot of Typical Farms in 1855   80
    Centers and Backwaters: Variation among Towns in 1855   86
    The Promise of Agricultural Life   93
    Politics and the Civil War   95

5   Dairy Farming, Commerce and Rural Industry 1865–1900   99
    Dairy Farming in Western New York   99
    A Portrait of Two Allegany Towns in 1875   102
    Commercial Growth in Fillmore and Wellsville   105
    Farmers and Village Merchants: Another Prisoner's
    Dilemma Game   109
    Maintaining Community Values   111
    Women's Role as Manager of the Home   116
    Manufacturing in Western New York Villages   120
    Political Party Competition: Rum, Romanism and Rebellion   124

6   The Automobile and Rural Decline: 1900–1950   126
    Quality of Rural Life   126
    The Decline of Dairy   129
    The Politics of Agricultural Decline   135
    Impact of the Automobile   138
    Housing Styles in the Automobile Age   141

7   Life in a Barely Agricultural Western New York: 1950–Present 146
    Changes in the Rural Economy   146
    Future of the Western New York Dairy Farm   150
    Population Trends in Allegany County   153
    Measuring Economic and Social Well Being   155
    The Automobile and Housing Patterns   157
    Local Political Issues in a Larger Society   164
    The Changing Landscape: From Pasture to Forest   171
    Today's Economic Challenges and Opportunities   178

Bibliography   183

Index   191

About the Author   195

Preface

This book offers an economic and political perspective on 200 years of social change in western New York. Data are taken primarily from Allegany County, and many people have helped me find material and interpret its significance. I am indebted to several of my colleagues at Alfred University. Mark McGovern, senior environmental studies major, mastered geographic systems technology and showed how land elevation and physical distance affected early settlement patterns. He also computerized data from the hand written 1855 census records, facilitating analysis of mid nineteenth century farm life. Professor Diana Sinton assisted McGovern in developing the GIS analysis, and taught me to appreciate the importance of geographic variables in social life.

Professor Cecelia Beach worked with students to translate 200 pages of Dupont family letters written from 1806-1809 from the original French. Professor Jim Booker in numerous conversations helped me to work out how transportation costs and economies of scale shaped economic decision making on the western New York frontier. Librarians at Alfred University and Alfred State College libraries guided me through their collections of historical material. I am particularly indebted to Laurie Mc Fadden. My fellow historians at the New York State Historical Association and the Pioneer America Society provided a sympathetic forum for some of the material.

Many Allegany County informants shared their local knowledge with me. Allegany County historian Craig Braack's knowledge of local history is truly encyclopedic. His many talks on Allegany County history have taught me much, and I thank him for our many conversations. He has steered me in the right direction, and his enthusiasm is contagious. Craig generously made available historic images of Allegany County from his personal post card collection. The staff at local libraries in Belfast, Bolivar, Fillmore and Wellsville helped me to find information that found its way into the book. Tom Parmenter and Elsworth Swift provided information and insight on the dairy industry, past and present.

Margaret Rasmussen has been a loyal, encouraging comrade and critic. Her skills as a trained historian have alerted me to flaws in evidence and interpretation, and she has generously applied her unparalleled editorial talents to the manuscript. The book is better organized and more readable as a result of her efforts. Personally, I can never thank her enough for being a warm companion during our years of marriage and for sharing with me her perspective on what's important.

I have lived a rewarding life in the midst of my fellow Allegany County citizens for 35 years. In respect and appreciation for their continuing effort to appreciate their past and shape their future, I dedicate this book to them.

Chapter One

Organizing Ideas: Central Place and Prisoner's Dilemma

When the first settlers arrived in western New York two centuries ago, they knew that years of back-breaking labor would provide only the most basic levels of food, clothing and shelter punctuated by periods of hunger and cold. They knew they might never see relatives left behind in New England and Pennsylvania. How the world has changed! National and international forces shape the everyday lives of regional residents; western New Yorkers listen to the same music, watch the same television programs, access the same internet, travel great distances via superhighways and airplanes, consume oil produced in the Middle East, wear clothes made in China, and eat wheat raised in Nebraska.

This book explores how and why economic fortunes, social life and political issues have changed over 200 years in western New York. Where did early settlers buy land and build their homes? Why did villages spring up in particular locations? Why did dairy farming replace mixed subsistence farming around 1850? Why did some villages prosper around 1900 while others stagnated? Why have so many factories in western New York closed their doors since World War II? Why has the political center shifted from county seat to state capital in Albany and to Washington DC?

THE IMPORTANCE OF TRANSPORTATION COSTS

Individuals hold down transportation costs and promote specialization and economies of scale to make more goods and services available at lower cost (Krugman 1955; Zipf 1949). This principle shaped behavior on the frontier farm in 1800, on the dairy farm after construction of the railroad in the 1850s, and in changing marketing and production patterns in the post World War II age of the automobile. Changing transportation costs, specialization and economies of scale help to explain social interaction patterns.

On the early nineteenth century frontier farm, taking horse and wagon to a village center four miles away was an exhausting half day trip that marked the effective limits of commercial activity. The center of the economy in western New York was the self-sufficient farm. Bringing in needed goods like coffee, candles and nails over rough forest paths was prohibitively expensive. So the frontier family did without coffee, dipped their own candles, and fashioned wooden pegs on winter evenings. Allegany County farmers originally built their homes near their fields rather than in villages to avoid transportation costs.

A half century later, when Genesee Valley Canal and the Erie Railroad connected Allegany County with Rochester, Buffalo and New York City, transportation costs fell sharply. Farmers had ready cash to spend as railroads carried their lumber and dairy products to eastern seaboard cities cheaply and quickly and shopkeepers brought construction material, hardware and consumer goods to the rural village. By 1900, farmers from a 15-mile radius could take the train or drive their wagons on improved roads to large regional villages like Hornell, Wellsville or Arcade and return the same day.

By 2008, the economic center has decisively shifted away from Arcade, Hornell and Wellsville to large cities like Buffalo and Rochester. Automobiles and televisions that Allegany County residents purchase are manufactured in distant places, and buyers easily drive 70 miles to an urban shopping mall to purchase goods and return home the same day. Local farms and factories withered under competition from large scale producers, and large commercial businesses based in cities increasingly offered goods and services at prices that village based stores could not match. The western New Yorker can reach much further in 2000 than an ancestor could in 1830. (See Table 1.1). As transportation has improved, people pursue more economic and social activities farther from home. People build their homes on lower-cost land along rural roads because their automobiles carry them quickly to neighboring villages and cities where they shop and work.

Table 1.1.

Year	Miles Traveled in 1 Hour	Method of Travel
1830	2	ox cart
1900	10	horse and buggy
1925	20	local railroad
2000	50	automobile

Source: Estimate for 1925 is taken from the Olean-Hornell railroad timetable. Other estimates are representative travel times in Allegany County.

Transportation is still costly, but when rural travelers arrive at the village or city, they find that the goods and services are worthwhile. That was true 200 years ago when small villages dotted the landscape and northern farmers lived within a few miles of the nearest village. It is true today, when good roads connect rural residents to a village 10 miles away and a super highway connects them to regional cities located 70 miles away.

SPECIALIZATION AND ECONOMIES OF SCALE

Carried to its limits, the idea that transportation is costly and, therefore, to be avoided would leave us as self-sufficient subsistence farmers, providing for all of our own needs (Cronon 1991; Krugman 1955). That is not true today, nor was it true for the first generation of settlers 200 years ago, who willingly traveled to their new homes on the frontier and then made periodic trips to the nearest village over difficult roads. People travel to take advantage of the fact that other people living in central places can provide goods and services more efficiently. Workers develop specialized skills that enable them to make horseshoes, tend to the sick or repair computers. When workers specialize, they can produce more and better goods and services. When they trade goods and services with other specialized workers, all enjoy higher standards of living. Specialization and economies of scale tend to concentrate production of goods and services in central places (Krugman 1955; Zipf 1949).

Several dozen villages dotted the Allegany County landscape in the early 1800s, and farmers gathered in those villages to make use of services they could not provide for themselves. In small villages like Angelica, Whitesville and Friendship, farmers sold their potash and surplus farm production and bought goods and services. Village centers were typically located seven miles apart along wagon paths, meaning that most farmers were no more than four miles from the closest village. The farm family could occasionally travel to the village; purchase supplies; talk with friends; and return home the same day without exhausting the horses that were needed for work the next day. Together, a community of people living within a four mile radius could build a school and hire a school teacher, pay a blacksmith to purchase tools and develop the skills to shoe horses or make barrel staves, and support a general store.

A century later, industrial and commercial production was well established in larger villages and regional cities of western New York. By 1900, specialization and economies of scale had transformed local economies. Producing to meet subsistence needs became part of the past. The years from about 1870 to 1920 marked the period of greatest prosperity in Allegany County, as state of the art factories converted farmers' milk into cheese that could be shipped on the railroad to distant urban consumers at low cost. Dairy farmers spent their cash in large regional villages that supported department stores, jewelers and bakers, banks and insurance agents. Some local workshops with one or two employees grew into small factories with a dozen or more employees. These factories typically transformed milk into cheese, hides into harnesses and timber into building materials.

Workers in factories and shops became more productive as fixed costs were spread over more units of production. Capital investment in processes that make a product faster and better costs less per unit of production if more units can be sold. A shopkeeper must keep his store open all day, and his labor costs or heating costs per dollar of sales are lower if he has 60 customers rather than 30. The cost of advertising to attract customers is less burdensome if daily sales are $200 rather than $100. Factories that produced goods for sale in distant markets expanded in rural western New York until about 1890, survived until about 1950, and closed down in the following decades.

Large factories and retail stores can manufacture and sell much larger quantities at low prices than could yesterday's small workshop or general store. By 2000, department stores, furniture stores and hardware stores in regional villages could no longer compete with malls located in regional cities like Buffalo and Rochester. At the mall, unique specialty stores like Starbucks or Old Navy, and high volume stores like Wal-Mart or Lowe's can provide wider selections at lower prices than stores in regional villages like Wellsville and Hornell. And the universe of the mail order catalog and online catalog shopping continues to expand.

Today, our social institutions have become even larger and more specialized. A small village of 250 people can't support a grocery store, auto repair shop or insurance agency, but a village of 2,500 can. That village of 2,500 can't support a hospital, a symphony orchestra or a Greek restaurant, but a city of 250,000 can. Large cities have flourished as locales where enough people live to support the production of specialized services such as brain surgery and live entertainment. In every twentieth century decade, the number of people choosing to live in large cities grows faster than the number living in small villages and rural areas.

Yet, the fortunes of town and country continue to be tied. Rural counties have fallen behind because urban areas typically produce goods more cheaply than do businesses located in rural areas. In cities, specialized computer services, advertising, office supplies and other services that businesses require are close at hand. Transportation costs are lower when businesses locate close to the raw materials they require or near their customer. Higher productivity in the cities means that firms can afford to pay their workers higher wages and rural customers are drawn from farm and village to the city. In the city, they purchase specialized medical services, see a ballet or professional sports team, or purchase big ticket items like automobiles, furniture and appliances.

POLITICS AND GAME THEORY

Changing transportation costs, economies of scale and specialization provide the context in which human social interactions take place, but they do not determine the choices that people make. Western New Yorkers, like people everywhere, seek to resolve differences in values and interests. In one common way of thinking about political competition, individuals are described as players in a game. Each player makes their best move, which determines who gets what in a world of scarce resources (Axelrod 1984; Ordeshook 1986). Native Americans and early settlers, dairy farmers and milk processing companies, shopkeepers and customers, husbands and wives, are viewed as players in a game, each trying to win in competition with other players.

Game theory assumes that players act rationally in pursuit of their self interest as they understand it. Each player seeks to earn the best possible score in the game. How a player scores depends upon the moves of the other player who has different goals in this competitive game. Individuals in all places and all times make the best decision available to them in the circumstances. So farmers in western New York decide exactly where to settle initially; whether to produce essential goods at home, barter with neighbors, or purchase goods at the general store in the nearest village; whether to practice mixed farming or to specialize in dairy production; whether to work on the farm or move to a regional village or city.

Some political conflicts are zero-sum games, like basketball or chess, where one person's gain just offsets another person's loss. A chess match or a baseball game with one winner and one loser is a zero-sum game. Politics is a zero-sum game when a Republican candidate for legislator defeats a Democratic opponent in the November election. If tax dollars are removed from one citizen's pocket and transferred to someone else's pocket, that outcome resembles a zero-sum game. Politics is also a zero-sum game when creditors on the frontier demand prompt payment on loans made to hard pressed borrowers. Politics is a zero-sum game when local citizens disagree on whether the county seat should be located in Angelica or Belmont, as they did in the 1850s. Or when temperance advocates win approval of a law banning the sale of alcohol which local drinkers oppose. In all of these settings, the gains to one player offset the losses to another.

More commonly, political conflicts are non-zero-sum games, when both sides win by cooperating together or lose by engaging in mutually destructive conflict. The Prisoner's Dilemma is a particularly common form of non-zero-sum game (Axelrod 1984). In a Prisoner's Dilemma game, a player can score very well (4 points) to very poorly (1 point). The outcome of the game depends upon whether each player decides to cooperate with (C) or defect on (D) the other player.

In the original Prisoner's Dilemma, the police arrest two players who they believe have committed a crime. The players are held in two separate rooms at the police station. Each prisoner has the option of cooperating with his comrade and not providing information to the police (C) or of defecting on his partner and confessing all to the police (D). If they each keep silent (C, C) the police can impose only a minor penalty and the prisoners will soon be free (3), a good outcome, given their situation. If one player keeps silent (C) while the other confesses (D), the police will throw the book at the silent prisoner (1), the worst possible outcome) and release the squealer immediately (4), his best possible outcome). If they both talk, each will be convicted of a lesser offense (2). Each player must choose whether to cooperate with his pal and keep silent about their activities or to squeal to the police and be set free for defecting on your partner-in-crime. Table 1.2 summarizes the result of this Prisoner's Dilemma game.

The Prisoner's Dilemma is that the best solution to the game is for each player to keep silent and look forward to a quick release (3, 3), but the likelihood is that the players will be stuck in the inferior lower right cell (2, 2). The reason is that whatever Prisoner II does, Prisoner I is better off defecting. If Prisoner II cooperates, Prisoner I scores better by defecting, receiving 4 points rather than 3 points. If Prisoner II defects, Prisoner I still does better to defect, receiving 2 points rather than 1 point. Whether Prisoner II cooperates or defects, Prisoner I is better off defecting. Both players are locked in a game of chronic defection, receiving only 2 points in a war of all against all.

The wickedness of the Prisoner's Dilemma is that, in a single play game, a prisoner is better off defecting regardless of whether the other prisoner defects or cooperates. Yet players in social games often find their way to cooperative behavior and the larger payoff of 3 points. How can we explain that

Table 1.2.   In the upper right cell, for example, if Prisoner I cooperates while Prisoner II defects, Prisoner I earns the worst possible score (1) and Prisoner II scores very well indeed (4).

		Prisoner II	
		C	D
Prisoner I	C	(3, 3)	(1, 4)
	D	(4, 1)	(2, 2)

players frequently cooperate, finding their way to the higher scoring (3, 3) outcome? If two players have a long future together, that is they will continually play their game for many rounds, cooperative behavior pays. A player has no incentive to defect on a cooperating player to achieve a short run gain (4 points rather than 3) if the wronged player will retaliate immediately, defecting back on the next move, each player now receiving only 2 points. In the new mood of distrust, each player can be trapped in a cycle of mutual defection, each player receiving only 2 points. When the players know that many moves remain in their game, they can find their way to cooperative behavior more easily. Neighbors on adjoining farms, husbands and wives in a continuing marriage, customers and shopkeeper whose store is a fixture in the community are players who expect to have a long future together. For these players, cooperation pays.

Relations among community members are often a non-zero-sum Prisoner's Dilemma game. Family members customarily build strong bonds with family members by sharing holiday meals and exchanging birthday cards or presents. Members of a community smile and say hello to one another on the street and help one another in time of need. As farm life has evolved over 200 years, rural Americans choose how to compete and cooperate with their neighbors. Young people seek desirable marriage partners; neighbors discuss their contributions to raising a barn or repairing a road. Neighbors participate in local parades and theater productions, and join baseball teams or coronet bands. They all benefit by observing customary rules and building strong ties with family and neighbors.

The interesting feature of Prisoner's Dilemma games is that players must continually decide whether or not to cooperate or defect on the other player. When are players likely to cooperate and avoid the lower scoring D/D outcome? First, the less likely it is that regular interactions will take place in the future, the less likely that players will develop the habit of cooperation. A local resident will treat an itinerant worker or traveling salesman with suspicion. Cultural distance between Native Americans and early settlers, between Protestant farmers and Irish Catholic laborers lead each player to conclude that he is better off defecting whatever the other player does. When regular interactions take place, each player can reward cooperating behavior and punish defecting behavior.

Second, the larger the social network, the greater is the temptation to defect by free riding on the efforts of others in the community (Olson 1965). Family bonds are tighter than bonds between members of the same community. Better roads were very much in every settler's interest, but individual settlers were reluctant to devote time and energy to road work that would mostly benefit others. Everyone hoped that they could ride free on the road improving efforts of their neighbors.

How do individuals overcome this free rider problem, which slowed the rate of socially desirable investment in better roads schools, and police protection? One strategy was for neighboring families to agree to do their fair share toward improving roads. Those who fulfilled their responsibility were well regarded by their neighbors, while those who shirked their community responsibility were criticized or shunned. As communities grow larger, neighborhood based social sanctions are less effective. The larger the group, the harder it is to detect free riding behavior and to sanction free riders. Early settlers, for example, had every reason to improve local roads to reduce their transportation costs, but each settler was tempted to do less than his fair share. Every subsequent traveler benefited from the efforts of the earliest settlers who hacked a road out of the forest, or removed fallen trees that blocked the road. But few bone-weary farmers would voluntarily work to improve roads that mostly benefited their neighbors. Each settler perceived that he was better off spending his time and energy clearing his own land. But if everyone thinks that way, the roads remain poor and everyone loses.

Similarly, dairy farmers might join a cartel to withhold milk from the market and drive up the price. If all farmers participate they might succeed in bidding up the price. But any individual farmer might hope that his boycotting neighbors continue to withhold supply, but decide to sell his own milk, thus undermining the boycott. Other farmers see that their neighbors are selling milk, realize that they are making a sacrifice to enrich others, and the boycott collapses.

To avoid this free rider problem, governments are given the authority to impose monetary or labor taxes so that all citizens are required to contribute to roads and schools that benefit all. Township or county government then paid workers to maintain and improve local roads. In 1800 when transportation costs were high and economies of scale limited, political competition over who gets what was exclusively local. Two hundred years later, when transportation costs are lower and economies of scale are great, most political decisions that affect Allegany County residents are made in Albany and Washington DC. As the population of western New York has stagnated, the region has lost political clout.

Third, in a Prisoner's Dilemma game, players have an incentive to hide their real preference. A local politician in 1910 might offer to surrender local control of school construction or road maintenance to the state government in Albany, but not if local taxes will increase to pay for improvements. Tom Sawyer reluctantly allows his neighbors to help him whitewash the fence, converting a favor he receives to a favor he bestows upon his helper. If a teenager expresses how badly he wants access to the car on Saturday night, his parents may require more timely and more spirited participation in completing chores around the house. Louis Paul d'Autremont, who financed his family's settlement in Angelica from Paris, illustrates the idea of strategic bargaining. To purchase land, he advises his mother, "I believe that if you are careful, you can buy land at $4.00 or $4.50 per acre. Alexandre (her son) has only to pretend not to care for them, and talk a great deal about buying other lands from Victor Dupont." (Louis Paul d'Autremont to his mother, July 27, 1806, P. 66).

An effective strategy for scoring as well as possible in a non-zero-sum game is tit for tat. When using tit for tat strategy, a player cooperates on the first move and then continues to cooperate if the other player cooperates, but defects immediately if the other player defects. If the other player then cooperates, you immediately follow suit. Several features make tit for tat an effective strategy in non-zero-sum game settings. First, the strategy is nice, in that the player is disposed to cooperate with others. Second, the strategy is easy to understand. Player A will follow whatever player B did on the previous move; if B cooperated, A will cooperate, if B defected, A will defect. Third, tit for tat is retaliatory; if B sneaks in a defection in order to make a short term gain (4), A immediately retaliates. B now receives 2 points, is no longer scoring as well as he would if he cooperated (3), and faces the possibility that a mistrustful A will continue to defect. Fourth, tit for tat is forgiving. If B offers to make peace by cooperating, A will immediately cooperate in return. Both players score 3, and are doing as well as they can in a competitive situation (Axelrod 1984, p. 8). Many historical interactions in western New York may be interpreted as two person non-zero-sum games, as we shall see in the following chapters.

Social relationships are fluid and reality is complex. This very simple model of human interaction as a game won't predict all human behavior accurately. It may well be that people in social interactions behave altruistically, without reference to their own self interest. Or their behavior may be guided by religious beliefs quite independent of any notion of self interest. If a parent gives his/her life for a child, this altruistic behavior does assure that ones genes live on, surely an important measure of personal success (Axelrod 1984, p. 89). Often societies promote the idea that the gods will approve behavior that promotes the ongoing well being of society and its members. Assuming that humans pursue their individual self interest simplifies complex reality to get to essential regularity in human behavior in many different settings in many different times. The more common it is that individuals pursue their self interest, the less it matters that a game model may not explain all individual behavior.

WHY FOCUS ON ONE WESTERN NEW YORK COUNTY?

Organizing ideas that are general enough to explain human behavior in many social settings at many different points in time are needed to answer these questions in a satisfactory way. Theoretical ideas should help us to understand human behavior on the 1800 frontier and in today's highly interdependent national society. Data taken from a single county, Allegany County, build an argument that applies more generally to western New York.

To the extent that simple concepts in economics and politics illuminate 200 years of social change in Allegany County, we can understand the lives of local people throughout western New York. Over 200 years, the social reality of rural Americans is that the intimate bonds of community have given way to the larger, impersonal bonds of society. Declining transportation costs and increasing economies of scale and specialization have generated this change. Politics continues to be a non-zero-sum game and rural Americans mistrust the large-scale political and economic organizations that increasingly dominate social life.

The behavior of any 40,000 people varies in response to changing technological, economic and political circumstances over 200 years. If transportation costs, economies of scale and a game theory of politics illuminate how scarce resources are allocated in this complex Southern Tier county, they will also illuminate the dynamics of social change elsewhere in western New York. This book argues that people everywhere are guided by the need to trade off the decentralizing transportation costs and centralizing economies of scale. Their political and social relations are guided by a calculus that is captured by the Prisoner's Dilemma game. These concepts travel well; they shed light on the behavior of individuals in many rural communities in many places and in many times.

Do very different rural places in western New York have anything in common? In one sense, every place is unique and defies easy generalization. Drawing upon the lives and behavior of one rural family would run the risk of generalizing to all families the eccentric experience of one family. The experience and behavior of two neighboring farm families is undoubtedly very different in important ways. The behavior of people in a river valley town will be different from people who live in a more isolated hill side town. The behavior of people in western New York differ, depending upon, say, their proximity to the Erie Canal.

Allegany County with about 40,000 residents is small enough to control many variables. The 29 towns of Allegany County share similar dates of original settlement, similar access to technology and commercial markets, an identical political context as components of Allegany County in New York

State, a remote location distant from the Erie Canal and the eastern seaboard cities, and similar soil and climate characteristics.

Yet, a county of 40,000 people is large enough to sample human diversity. The 29 towns into which Allegany County is divided reveal a great deal of variation. The hills of Allegany County are drained by three major river systems, which enables us to test hypotheses about the effect of transportation costs on human settlement patterns. Allegany County also illustrates that county level data miss important variation in local experience. County level data are inevitably statistical averages with large standard deviations. Social change proceeded at a very different pace among Allegany County's 29 towns and 38 principal villages. Early settlers found that some towns were more attractive than others. The timing of transition from lumbering to dairy farming in Allegany County varied from town to town. Town and village level data available in local commercial directories enable us to reproduce the social structure of specific villages at a given point in time and show how social structure changed over several decades.

This book attempts to account for this variation in terms of differing transportation costs and economies of scale, and how people choose to play their Prisoner's Dilemma games in one complex western New York county over a 200-year time span. Earlier histories have not analyzed large amounts of census data available at the county and town level in western New York since 1855 have not been analyzed in a systematic way. Using these data, we can take a snapshot of social life at a given point in time. For example, census material reveals who lived in specific western New York farm households, where they were born, and how they earned their living. These sources show how individuals in different settings responded to broad historical trends. This book also draws upon much empirical information from commercial directories and satellite imaging. This information is a valuable supplement to many general regional histories that provide much of our knowledge about life in nineteenth century western New York. (Gates 1960; Mau 1944; McNall 1952).

In *Ox Cart to Automobile: Social Change in Western New York*, two central organizing ideas, central place theory and the Prisoner's Dilemma, illuminate 200 years of rural western New York history. These ideas are theoretically rich—they help us to understand individual behavior and social change in 1808 and in 2008. Each chapter explores several dimensions of social change in western New York.

One dimension is the interaction of physical landscape and social change. Glaciers shaped the physical environment in western New York during the ice age, and they also shaped the land use decisions of eighteenth century Native Americans, early nineteenth century settlers, and twentieth century dairy farmers. Early settlers cleared the forests to plant crops and twentieth century dairy farmers have abandoned their pastures, allowing the trees to cover the landscape once again.

How the role of women in rural western New York has evolved over this 200-year period is another important dimension. The Prisoner's Dilemma illuminates resources available to women in the frontier cabin, on the nineteenth century dairy farm, in the village workplace about 1900 and in the post World War II age of the automobile.

Domestic architecture reflects the economic position of families and changing ideas and technology. In the 1820s, for example, Greek revival expressed male political equality; in the 1890s, Queen Anne houses showcased village prosperity and new ideas about homemaking; the bungalow in the 1920s reflected a new interest in labor saving and convenience within the home; the ranch home and the trailer in the 1950s emerged because families in their automobile could easily access low cost land on abandoned farms.

The center of political life shifted from the local town hall in 1820 to Albany and Washington DC in 2008. Moral sensibility more than economic self interest has shaped political allegiances to Republican and Democratic parties in different generations. In 1820, temperance and evangelical Protestantism were the moral concern. In 1860 slavery, in 1900 the corruption of the city and in recent decades the threat of big government in Albany and Washington to rural and small town traditions has shaped political life in western New York.

Chapter Two

Distance, Elevation and Early Settlement Decisions

All human inhabitants of Allegany County, including small numbers of Native Americans living along the Genesee or passing through the area to trade with or raid more distant Indian communities; white settlers who moved into the area from Pennsylvania and New England; and contemporary Allegany County residents, have adapted to the same geologic setting. The 200 years since the formation of Allegany County are but a geologic instant. The hills and valleys that we know today are the same hills and valleys that shaped the lives of the earliest settlers. Yet, over 200 years the economic and social meaning of the physical landscape has changed dramatically, as examined in this chapter.

THE LEGACY OF ROCKS AND ICE

Road, rail and stream cuts in western New York reveal up to 100 feet of alternating layers of Devonian shales, sandstone and limestone deposited about 300 million years ago (Woodruff 1942). Long before the first glacial ice sheets spread over western New York about 18,000 years ago, a warm shallow sea covered most of the Southern Tier. This sea was home to many invertebrates, which formed layers of limestone embedded with abundant fossil shells. Also, layers of fine silt formed shale and layers of sand were compressed into sedimentary rock. Later, these layers of limestone, shale and sedimentary rock were uplifted into the hills that dominate the Southern Tier landscape today. Over many thousands of years, rain eroded these high hills, attacking the least resistant rock and creating the ridge pattern that defines today's Allegany County landscape. In general, major Allegany County roads and state highways today follow paths through the valleys and around the ends of hills. These valleys today contain roads and fertile fields, but they once contained the melt waters of the glaciers. The Genesee River once filled the entire valley formed by the hills on either side of the river.

The glaciers flowed through valleys, following the path of least resistance. As the glaciers flowed, they did the work of huge bulldozers, transporting rocks and boulders long distances, grinding them down into sand and gravel, and reshaping the Allegany County landscape. Along the creeks, ice towered 1000 feet over the land surface. The upper ice flowed over the local bedrock, rounding the typical hill into its shape today. The tremendous weight of the ice pushed the hills down, and today the land continues to rebound at the rate of several inches per year. The southward flowing ice bulldozed huge quantities of earth and rock. The limestone rock that fills the local farmer's fields and lines creek beds is not native to Allegany County but originated near Lake Ontario. When the glaciers began their retreat, they left behind landscape-transforming quantities of glacial debris, or till. The bedrock of Allegany County ridges is buried in three to 10 feet of gravel, stones and boulders left behind by the retreating glaciers. On the valley floors, bedrock is buried in up to 300 feet of dirt, gravel and sand. These broad, flat valleys are more fertile than are eroded hillsides and glacier-scoured hilltops (Cressey 1966).

Walking along an Allegany County creek, you are standing on layers of glacial till deposited by melting glaciers. The creeks have been cutting away at the glacial till for about 6000 years, carrying off the small particles of sand and gravel and leaving behind larger limestone rocks that now fill the creek beds. The valleys are wide because they were carved out by glacier ice and subsequent erosion by massive rivers and streams. Rivers and creeks are quite small, or "under fit" as geologists say, in comparison to the huge glacial rivers that shaped the larger Allegany County landscape. As the rivers flowed to the sea, they deposited huge amounts of sand and silt on the valley floors, creating the area's best agricultural land.

Many features of the contemporary western New York landscape are the product of water running along the retreating glaciers. On the glacier, pockets of dark rocks and soil absorbed the sun's heat, melting the adjacent ice at a faster rate and allowing rivers to form on the surface of the glacier. Over hundreds of years, these glacial rivers deposited layers of sand and gravel that remain long after the ice has melted. What remains today is a snake-like ridge, an esker, winding along the surface of the land. The hills on both sides of Route 36 are kame terraces, sand and gravel deposited by rivers that flowed along the surface of the glacier that filled Whitney Valley. These sand and gravel deposits are today an important economic resource. The kame terraces along the east edge of a north/south running valley are larger in size because warm afternoon temperatures and direct afternoon sun increased the melt rate.

When the southward flow of the ice balanced the rate at which the ice was melting, glacial till would accumulate in an east/west ridge called a moraine. Kettles, rounded depressions in the landscape, were created when a stream flowing along the surface of the glacial ice encountered an erosion resistant block of ice. As the water slowed to flow around this erosion resistant block of ice, it deposited sand around the perimeter. Finally, the block of ice melted, leaving a nicely rounded depression (Matsch 1976). Some valleys in glacial times contained great lakes. The rich agricultural fields north of Arkport are a notable example. Karr Valley near Almond was originally a lake blocked by Sand Hill until the water cut an outlet at the ledges (Reynolds 1962). In the Alfred area, a glacial lake deposited today's clay and shale surface material.

WHERE DID EARLY MIGRANTS CHOOSE TO SETTLE?

The hilly terrain shaped by the ancient glaciers and heavily forested in 1800 provided a difficult environment for early settlers. Following the revolutionary war, settlers from New England and Pennsylvania moved westward into eastern and central New York in large numbers. The first settler walked into Allegany County in 1795, and by 1810, about 1200 families were hard at work carving homesteads out of the forest. Where did these migrants decide to settle and why? In the absence of a reason to prefer one location to another, we would expect settlers to distribute themselves uniformly over the landscape. All towns in the county would be settled in similar numbers at about the same time. But early settlers did appear to favor some areas over others. Three alternative hypotheses are considered that might account for differences in early settlement patterns.

First, newcomers may have settled where other family and former neighbors from back east had already made their homes. Earlier pioneers could provide newcomers with advice, assistance and comfort. Second, migrants may have preferred to settle close to Bath and Batavia, the dominant market towns in the region. That would lower the costs to settlers of importing goods they could not easily make themselves, enable them to export potash and goods they produced in their homes and on their farms, and facilitate communicating with family and friends back east. Third, settlers might have preferred either low or high elevation lands. Low elevation river valleys had the advantage of richer soils, longer growing seasons and more level terrain to ease the burdens of travel. On the other hand, higher elevation lands were easier to clear and free of disease carrying insects that inhabited the lowlands. McNall writes, "Narrow valleys were susceptible to freshets and heavy spring floods. The denser forests of the valleys with heavily rooted, moisture loving trees and matted small vegetation retained water and rendered the clearing process difficult. Better drainage made the hills more easily prepared for the plow" (McNall 1952, p. 82).

Does evidence support any of these hypotheses? To answer this question, we draw upon early population distribution data for the 29 towns in Allegany County, farm location data from Beer's 1869 Atlas, and elevation data using contemporary satellite imaging.[1] Because of its diverse physical characteristics, Allegany County is an excellent research setting. Its hilly terrain drains into three river systems, the Susquehanna River to the east, the Genesee River to the north and the Allegheny River to the west. The first immigrants followed the Susquehanna River from Pennsylvania, arriving in Allegany County at the turn of the nineteenth century. Many immigrants from New England soon followed. Learning where and why early Allegany County settlers decided to locate will help us to understand the dynamics of settlement elsewhere on the western New York frontier. Traditionally, historians have used countywide data extensively to tell the story of nineteenth century settlement in western New York (Miller, 1979; Parkerson, 1995; Tryon, 1917). But county level data obscure considerable economic and social variation within a given county. Town and local level data reveal patterns that are invisible when data are aggregated at the county level (Rasmussen, 2000).

We first need to establish whether early settlers distributed themselves uniformly across the landscape or whether they preferred some local settings to others. Note that the earliest settlers arrived in the 29 Allegany towns at quite different times. Map 2.1 shows that the first permanent settlers arrived in 14 towns between 1795 and 1808. Settlers broke ground in the remaining 13 towns between 1816 and 1833, with the exception of Wirt in 1812 (Minard 1896, p. 322). Settlers were reluctant to move into new areas between 1808 and 1816 because of the threat of hostilities with England and her Indian allies in the years before and after the war of 1812 (Mau 1944, p. 197). So some Allegany County towns were opened up a whole generation earlier than others.

Population in Allegany County grew rapidly between 1810 and 1850, from 1,200 to 40,000 inhabitants, as Table 2.1 shows. Did the newcomers prefer to settle in some towns rather than others?

Table 2.1.   Allegany County Population, 1810-1850

Year	Population
1810	1200
1820	5400
1830	20000
1840	30000
1850	40000

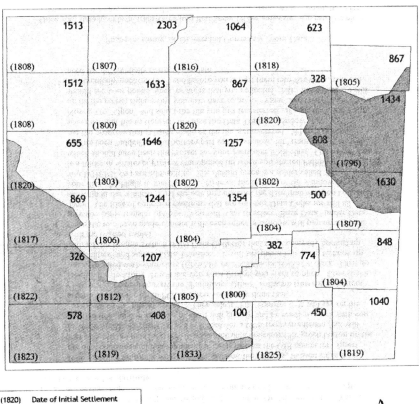

(1820) Date of Initial Settlement
450 Estimated 1840 Population
Genesee watershed
Allegany watershed
Upper Susquehanna watershed

0   4   8   12 Miles

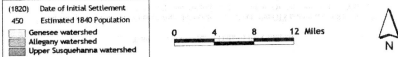

N

Map 2.1.   County Watersheds and Town Divisions with Date of Initial Settlement and Estimated 1840 Population, Allegany County New York.

As settlers moved into the county between 1810 and 1850, the original six towns were split into smaller ones in order to tax and to provide government services more effectively. Population for towns that did not exist in 1840 was estimated on the basis of their 1865 populations and a comparison of similar towns with known 1840 populations. The numbers were then subtracted from the reported populations of towns that gave up territory to the new towns. In 1850, Allegany County was fully populated, in the sense that population held constant at about 40,000 people for the next 100 years. Map 2.2 shows that population in 1820 was not spread evenly across the six original towns.

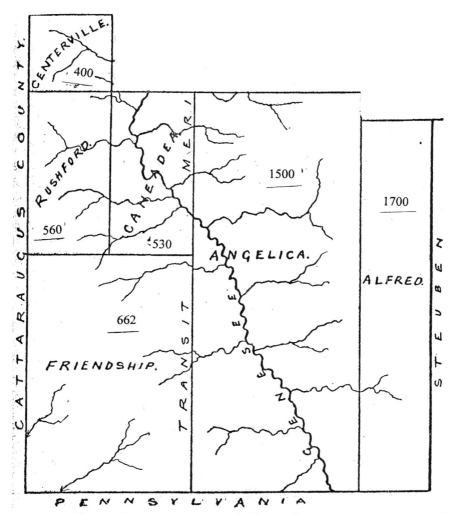

Map 2.2.   Allegany County 1820, Town Divisions and Population. Source: Minard 1896, p. 83.

The boundary of Alfred town runs along the ridge of hills that separate the Susquehanna and Genesee river basins. Although not large in size, Alfred town was home to about 1700 inhabitants in 1820, nearly 30 percent of the total county population. The town of Angelica, including most of the Genesee River Valley, had some 1500 inhabitants. Angelica grew rapidly after completion of the Erie Canal in 1825 shifted Allegany County's economic center of gravity from Alfred town and the Susquehanna River valley to the

Erie Canal and the booming economic centers of Rochester and Buffalo. By 1840, the four largest towns with populations around 1700—Hume, Belfast, Cuba and Caneadea—were located in the Genesee Valley.

The large town of Friendship, including the Allegheny River basin, had only about 660 inhabitants in 1820. Most of these settlers were clearing land in the northeast hills drained by the Genesee. Southwest towns drain into the Allegheny River, which joins the Ohio at Pittsburgh. The Allegheny River system was of little use except as a transportation route to newly opened lands in Ohio and the west. The Allegheny mountains were a barrier to the south, and Pittsburgh was a frontier outpost, not an economic center. Since the date of initial settlement and population in 1820 varied considerably among Allegany County towns, it is clear that early settlers did not distribute themselves randomly across the landscape.

FRIENDS, NEIGHBORS, AND EARLY SETTLEMENT

Why did settlers prefer some locations to others? If the first hypothesis has merit, that settlers preferred areas where relatives, old friends, or new neighbors might provide comfort, advice and assistance, towns settled earliest should have larger populations in 1840 than did towns settled later. Newcomers would join the original core population. Neighbors could join together at barn raisings and quilting bees to make the work lighter. Together they could support a church and school, a blacksmith and a village store.

In general, towns settled at an early date lie in the Susquehanna River basin and along the Genesee River valley. Statistical analysis demonstrates that towns settled earliest continued to attract new settlers. The correlation between the date of initial settlement and town population in 1840 is -.34, controlling for distance and elevation.[2]

Before 1825, the Susquehanna River provided transportation of goods, primarily logs and potash, to major urban markets. Logs bound together formed rafts to carry goods to the major Atlantic ports in eight to ten days. Commercial prophets of the time pointed to the Susquehanna as "the destined highway of the West" (Beers, 1869). After completion of the Erie Canal in 1825, the county's economic center shifted to the Genesee River Valley. Allegheny River towns were settled at a later date and had smaller populations in 1840. Settlers who moved into Allegany County between 1810 and 1840 preferred the same Susquehanna and Genesee river basin towns.

To illustrate, six townships were selected based on their settlement date and their geographic locations in major river systems (Table 2.2). The settlers who poured into Allegany County between 1810 and 1840 faced the same

Table 2.2.   Initial Settlement Date and 1840 Population, Six Allegany County Towns

Town	Initial Settlement Date	1840 Population
Alfred	1807	1630
Amity	1804	1354
Centerville	1808	1513
Cuba	1817	869
Grove	1818	623
Bolivar	1819	408

transportation constraints as did the very first settlers. The towns of Alfred, Amity and Centerville that were settled early also had larger populations in 1840 than did the late settled towns of Grove, Cuba and Bolivar.

The town of Alfred is located 30 miles from Bath, a village at the head of the Susquehanna River and a center of early land sales in the region. Early settlers followed stream valleys to their new homes. The Genesee River flows northward through the center of the county, emptying into Lake Ontario. Completion of the Erie Canal in 1825 shifted Allegany County's center of gravity from Alfred town and the Susquehanna River valley to Amity and other Genesee River valley towns with access to the Erie Canal and the growing cities of Rochester and Buffalo. The Erie Canal reduced transportation costs by a factor of 10, and all of the Genesee River valley towns grew rapidly.

Location in the river valley system helps to explain differences in date of initial settlement and town population in 1840 among Allegany County towns. Early settlers largely ignored Bolivar and other Allegany River towns that were distant from Bath and other market villages. Poor roads and hilly terrain made transportation costs prohibitive. A group of Allegany County settlers complained to the Holland Land Company about the lack of roads, "There is a very respectable settlement of industrious settlers . . . who have, like resolute pioneers, broke the way far into the thick forest—and having no mills or public accommodations within a great distance they are under the necessity of traveling far, thro very bad roads or rather paths—and the intervening hills and gulphs are such as to make it very expensive, much more than individuals are able to bear" (Brooks 1996, p. 115).

EARLY FARMS AND DISTANCE FROM COMMERCIAL CENTERS

Our second hypothesis is that settlers preferred those river valley systems that were closer to large market villages in the region where transportation costs were lower. Location decisions were shaped largely by transportation costs on the frontier, primarily proximity to waterways that provided access to the interior and the means to ship goods between farm and market (Richardson 1973). Early settlers preferred to locate in areas with easy access to market towns, and travel was easier along the flat valleys carved out by rivers and streams.

Victor and Josephine Dupont, early settlers whose correspondence has survived, recorded the difficulties of travel on the frontier in 1806.[3] Josephine wrote from their new home in Angelica, "We no longer have to deal with the mountains, the abominable wilderness, the 40 horrid miles from Bath to here. This trip gave us a lot of difficulties I assure you, and this short route that my husband invented is really only passable in good weather and with wagons much less laden than ours, You have no idea what these miles were like." (Josephine to Mrs. Manigault, W3-4939, November 20 1806). Victor wrote to his brother, "An old man supported my wagon with a cord to prevent it from overturning. John did the same to the other wagon. The horses had an incredible amount of courage and strength. The drivers were very skillful and still more lucky because twenty times an hour we almost turned over, swallowed up by mud holes, the wheels nearly breaking against rocks or stumps. We climbed almost up for almost three miles, stopping every 10 steps to catch our breath." (Victor to Eleuthiere, W3-684, November 9, 1806).

The hypothesis that settlers preferred river valley locations closer to regional markets is tested statistically by measuring the distance from the largest, most centrally located village in each town to the county boundary nearest Bath and Batavia, the closest regional economic centers in the Susquehanna and Genesee River valleys. Bath was the principal gateway to the east for Allegany County in 1820. Batavia was closer for settlers located in Allegany County towns to the north and west. Greater distances from these market villages meant higher transportation costs. We expect that towns located closer to regional economic centers were more attractive to settlers than more distant towns. Before roads were improved, transporting 800 pounds of goods by oxen and wagon a distance of 12 miles required two or three days. The costs of shipping potash, lumber or farm crops to the outside world ate up the profits of farmers whose competitors worked closer to markets along Lake Erie.

The evidence supports the idea that settlers preferred locations closer to regional market towns. The statistical line of best fit shows that, about 1820, towns whose largest village was close to Bath or Batavia had larger populations; more distant towns had smaller populations. After completion of the Erie Canal in 1825, farmers in northern towns gained further advantage; farmers in southern Allegany towns had to pay an additional transportation cost to reach Erie Canal markets. Because of the cost premium associated with an additional 20 or 30 miles to market, after 1825 northern Allegany towns gained population more rapidly than towns in the southern part of the county.

ELEVATION AND EARLY SETTLEMENT

The third hypothesis is that, within each town, early settlers preferred to build their homesteads at lower elevations. Valley bottom soils were richer, the growing season longer and level land easier to work. At higher elevations in the Southern Tier, growing seasons were shorter than in the low-lying valleys. In high elevation areas with poor access to markets and fragile soils, farmers struggled compared to valley farmers who benefited from access to markets and more fertile soils (Huston 2000, p. 9). However, narrow valleys were susceptible to spring flooding, clearing valley floors with heavily rooted, moisture-loving trees was difficult and valley drainage was often poor (McNall 1952 p. 82).

Transportation costs are lower along flat river valleys than on hilly upland holdings. The first settlers moved into western New York along the river valleys, and the small villages that sprang up as commercial centers for the surrounding farms are located along rivers and streams. Most villages are located on rivers and streams.

That households tended to be located at lower elevations can be shown precisely with Geographic Information Systems (GIS) technology. Households noted in the D.G. Beers 1869 Atlas of Allegany County were located in relation to roads, streams and lot lines. Since Allegany County was fully populated in 1840, most of the farms that appear in Beer's 1869 Atlas were already established in 1840. Each household was then transcribed onto a digital map and placed over a 10-meter digital elevation grid for each town. Think of this process as placing a pin representing household location on a digital elevation grid layer. The pinpoint then lands in a 10-meter grid cell and its elevation is noted. Map 2.3 illustrates the results for the town of Bolivar when household location is superimposed over a topographic map showing elevations, roads and streams. Some cash poor settlers preferred lower cost land at higher elevations. Also, labor short households may have preferred to clear less densely wooded sites.

To illustrate the impact of elevation on settlement patterns, we compare expected and observed house counts for six geographically diverse towns. The expected house count is based on the percentage of 10-meter grid cells in the entire landscape. If 20 percent of the 10-meter grid cells fell within the 451-500 meter range, random distribution would place 20 percent of the house-

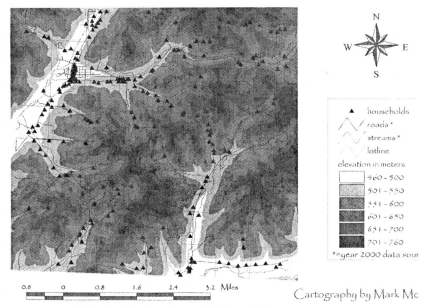

N
W — E
S

▲ households
roads *
streams *
lotline
elevation in meters
460 - 500
501 - 550
551 - 600
601 - 650
651 - 700
701 - 760
*=year 2000 data sour

0.8   0   0.8   1.6   2.4   3.2 Miles

Cartography by Mark Mc

Map 2.3.   Household Distribution, Town of Bolivar 1869.
Source: McGovern and Rasmussen, 2003.

holds in the 451–500 meter range. The observed house count presents the actual number of houses in each elevation range. For each town, the relationship between elevation and settlement patterns is presented. In general, households in 1869 were concentrated at lower elevations and along roads. Very few households were located at higher elevations over 651 feet.

The town of Alfred, for example, is located on the eastern border of the county in the Susquehanna River valley. The topography consists of irregular hills with elevations up to 740 meters above sea level and deep narrow valleys with elevations in the 440-550 meter range. The picture above represents the distribution of households in Alfred among the various elevation ranges. The lighter cones represent the actual number of households observed in each elevation range. The darker cones represent the expected number of households in the elevation range, based on the percentage of 10-meter grid cells in the entire landscape. Forty percent of households were located in the low-lying 440-550 meter elevation range. Only 19 per cent of the total landscape is contained in this same range. By locating at lower elevations, settlers avoided the hardships of transporting goods up and down hills. Additionally, having easier access to the village of Alfred made possible more social interaction.

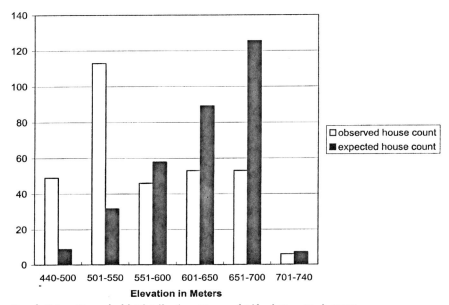

Graph 2.1.   Household Distribution, Town of Alfred New York 1869.

The largest percentage of the Alfred landscape falls in the 651-700 meter range. If household distribution were random, the largest percentage of observed household counts would also fall in this range. Clearly this was not the case; household distribution was concentrated in the 501-550 meter range. Early settlers most likely chose to locate in the lower valley elevations; later arrivals to Alfred were forced to locate in the higher elevations. Also, the fact that over 87 percent of the landscape elevation of Alfred falls above 550 meters may explain the concentration of households in the village.

The strongest association between elevation and household distribution (.734) is found in the town of Amity. The Genesee River runs through a wide fertile valley and provided power for mills and transportation of logs to markets in the city of Rochester. Only 27 percent of the landscape of Amity falls within the low 400-450 meter range of the Genesee River valley, but nearly 80 percent of the households were located there.

The town of Bolivar is isolated in the southwestern corner of the county. Bolivar's landscape is hilly, and over 54 percent of the landscape lies above 601 meters. Only 17 percent of households were located in high elevation areas. Conversely, only seven percent of the town lies below 500 meters, but 35 percent of the households are located in this range. Farming was easier in the low elevation valleys, and the village of Bolivar closer.

Elevation also influenced household location and transportation routes in Cuba. Settlers favored the wide, flat valley that runs north/south through the center of the town. Railroad and canal ran through this wide valley in the 1850s. Flat land reduces transportation costs, whether moving household belongings by horse or foot or when moving massive loads by steam. The low 450-500 meter elevation range in Cuba represents 24 percent of the landscape; yet, 70 per cent of the households were located within this range.

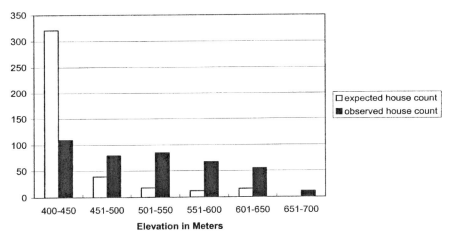

Graph 2.2.   Household Distribution, Town of Amity New York 1869.

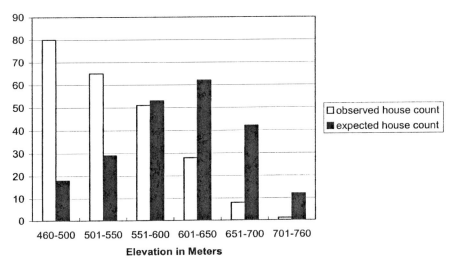

Graph 2.3.   Household Distribution, Town of Bolivar New York 1869.

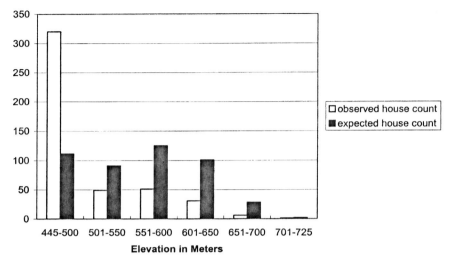

Graph 2.4.   Household Distribution, Town of Cuba New York 1869.

In the town of Centerville, located in the northernmost part of Allegany County, grade changes are less steep. Wide expanses of gradual slopes stretch across the landscape, as opposed to the steep grade changes typical of Alfred and Bolivar. Household distribution in Alfred, Amity and Bolivar was concentrated in the lower elevations, but Centerville's household distribution approaches randomness. The weakest association between household distribution and elevation, a Goodman-Kruskal statistic of .186, was found in Centerville. The gently rolling terrain and lack of a major waterway account for this weak association between elevation and population. The household distribution chart shows that household distribution follows the roads and that the observed and expected counts in Centerville are very close for each elevation range. When steep grade changes did not require curving roads through the valley, roads were laid out in a balanced grid with right angles at intersections. In the southern part of the county, roads wind around severe grade changes. Most Centerville roads follow a straight line across the gentle changes in grade. Many of these roads are oriented directly north/south or east/west.

The distribution of households in Grove in 1869 resembles that of Centerville. Grove lacked a major river for transport or power. The distribution is almost random, although again, the observed house count exceeds the expected in the lower elevations. As in Centerville, houses were distributed in a semi-geometric pattern along side roads that are oriented at right angles to each other.

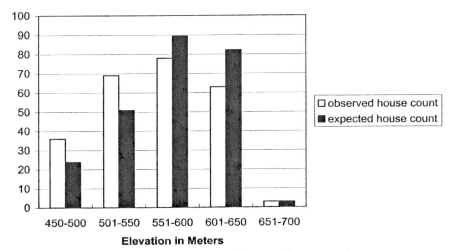

Graph 2.5. Household Distribution, Town of Centerville New York 1869.

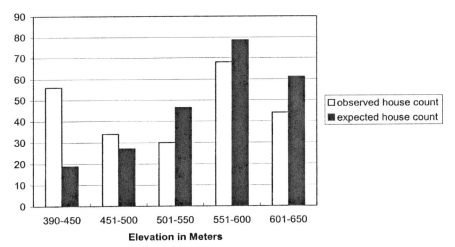

Graph 2.6. Household Distribution, Town of Grove New York 1869.

For each of these six towns, household distribution is concentrated in the lower elevation ranges.

Statistical analysis for 29 towns supports three hypotheses concerning why early settlers located where they did. They settled where others had come before, they located near regional market towns and they built their homesteads at lower elevations.[4]

LOCAL VILLAGES AS CENTRAL PLACES

Early nineteenth century settlers tended to carve out their farms in close proximity to earlier migrants in order to provide collective goods and to achieve
economies of scale. Life on the frontier was nasty, brutish and lonely, and
early settlers preferred to clear land in or near villages for security in a trou-
bled times, social companionship and easy access to school and church,
blacksmith shop and general store. New settlers followed friends and relatives who had already established new lives in Allegany County. About 1820,
at least 32 population centers had emerged at intersections of streams and
trails in Allegany County, and no farmer was more than four miles away from
one of these population centers (Rasmussen 2001). These villages supported
about nine gristmills, 22 sawmills and five asheries (Spafford 1981).

Beers prepared detailed village population maps in 1869 for each of the
largest 32 villages. My count of his stores and houses suggests that about 20
per cent of Allegany County population lived within these 32 villages in
1869. Forty years earlier, the population living in villages was probably similar. One local historian estimates that the village of Almond, for example,
contained 60 dwellings and 400 people in 1842 (Minard 1896, p. 566). Assuming that 12 larger villages averaged about 400 inhabitants and 20 smaller
ones averaged about 200 in 1840, about one person in five lived in villages in
Allegany County in 1830.

Many village dwellers were primarily farmers. Land was typically sold in
rectangular plots with the narrow end along roads and stream and the long
end extending uphill. Farmers grew crops and pastured animals on their fields
that extended up the hillsides from their homes along Main Street. Today,
many barns have been converted to garage and storage area but still remain
behind Main Street houses in Allegany County villages.

Villages were located astride the roads that ran along valley floors. The
mean distance between 32 neighboring villages was seven miles (Beers
1869). Most early farmers could travel to town and return home in less than
a day. Farmers quickly saw that they were better off selling felled logs,
potash, surplus animals and bushels of grain to purchase the services of blacksmith, sawmill and carpenter in the nearby village. Self-sufficiency was
costly, as settlers had neither the equipment nor the skill to manufacture a
wide variety of household needs at home. Mill operators and skilled craftsmen produced better goods at a fraction of the cost. Farmers quickly gave up
fashioning nails at home on long winter nights once blacksmith with a forge
and anvil located in the village three miles away.

To the extent that a farm family could generate cash from the sale of lumber or potash, a surplus cow or a few bushels of grain, the family avoided the

arduous labor of fashioning their own rough cloth, shoes and candles. The women of the household benefited mightily from additional household income, being spared time consuming hand manufacture of objects offered for sale at the general store.

Cash was hard to come by for the farm family on the frontier, and the trees they cut were the most likely source of family income. Most early settlers chose locations in the Susquehanna River basin along the eastern edge of Allegany County. During the winter months, settlers cut trees, skidded them down the frozen hill to the creek, and built a flat-bottomed boat. Flat-bottomed arks drawing two feet of water could transport 1200 bushels of wheat or 20 tons of lumber during periods of high stream flow. Early settlers loaded the ark with lumber or potash and floated down the creek on the spring flood to the Canisteo/Susquehanna River to the Chesapeake Bay (McNall 1952). There they found a ready market for lumber among well established communities that had already exhausted local supplies of timber. The Steuben County village of Arkport takes its name from this early economic activity. Two workers could construct an ark in two weeks. The 350-mile trip down the Susquehanna to Baltimore took six days and the attention of a crew of four. After dismantling the ark and selling the lumber, the crew walked back to Allegany County. The river was a one way street, suitable for transporting lumber and wheat downstream but not very useful for transporting consumer goods northward.

When the Erie Canal was completed in 1825, the center of lumbering in Allegany County shifted to the Genesee River Valley. In the 1830s and 1840s, ox drawn wagons hauled lumber along present day Route 36 to Mount Morris below Letchworth Falls, where the cargo was transferred to rafts and shipped to Rochester and the Erie Canal. Residents of Centerville, Granger, Grove and other northern Allegany towns hauled their wagon loads to Dansville or Canandaigua or Buffalo, depending upon distance, road conditions and market prices.

The village of Belfast was the center of Genesee River rafting. During the fall and winter, logs were cut and skidded to the river bank. In the spring, the logs, bearing the owner's brand, were floated to large sawmills at Portageville and Mount Morris. The difficult and dangerous work of breaking up logjams along the way gave rise to our saying, "As easy as falling off a log." Downstream, the logs were stored in booms along the shore, out of the main stream flow, and eventually fed to the saw mill (Wood 1971).

Shipping low value, unprocessed logs by team on rough roads was not a very profitable activity in 1825. Local Allegany county settlers had built about 22 sawmills to reduce weight and bulk while creating a more valuable product, sawn boards (Spafford 1981). Land companies, desiring to make an area more attractive to prospective settlers, provided free land or other subsidies to saw mill operators and other artisans willing to set up operations in a lightly populated area. Perhaps the earliest sawmill in Allegany County was constructed on Wiscoy Creek in 1807.

Mill construction techniques were old and well established. A sudden drop of 10 to 15 feet was needed to turn the mill wheel. To create that drop, water was diverted into a mill race from an upstream high point to the wheel downstream. A dam upstream elevated the water several feet (Wallace 1978). A wooden wheel driven by the weight of water turned gears that communicated power to mill machinery—a saw blade or mill stones to convert corn or wheat into flour. Wheels were typically 10 to 15 feet in diameter and 3 or 4 feet wide. The water constantly sought a way around the dam and flash floods were a perennial problem along mill streams. Progressive deforestation of the hillsides speeded runoff, threatening dam and the mill downstream.

In the 1820s and 1830s, groups of Allegany County men migrated north with their scythes to assist lower Genesee Valley farmers harvest their wheat. The short growing season in Allegany's elevated plateau made wheat growing difficult, and in a good crop year, local farmers could not afford to transport their wheat surplus to urban markets. For these Allegany County migratory workers, seasonal labor was more attractive than hauling lumber over impassable roads (Merrill 1908).

ROAD BUILDING IN ALLEGANY COUNTY

Major roads in Allegany County today follow the valleys carved by the Genesee River and the various creeks that feed the Susquehanna, Genesee and Allegheny Rivers. The first road in Allegany County followed Nathaniel Dyke's trail from Hornell through Whitney Valley to Andover and then westward along Dyke Creek to the Genesee River at Wellsville. Most settlers, seeking to minimize their transportation costs, built roads that wound through the valleys carved by the glaciers. The earliest settlers in the Almond area turned up Karr Valley, and Philip Church initially followed Karr Valley to his holdings in Angelica (Reynolds 1962, p. 74).

The principal exception to the rule that roads follow the valley floors, the ridge road between Karr and McHenry Valleys, was built by Philip Church as a major turnpike in 1810 and 1811. After purchasing provisions in Geneva, Church proceeded to Almond. When his crews built Turnpike Road to connect Almond and Angelica, they followed not the Karr Valley path but chose a route high on a ridge about a mile south of Karr Valley Road. But within 20 years, Karr Valley settlers had cleared the land and dried out the swamp. They built the road to Angelica, the county seat and gateway to the Genesee, and Turnpike road fell into disuse.

Why had Turnpike Road initially been built along the top of the ridge? Turnpike Road builders sought to build access between Angelica and Almond, not to open up the wilderness. They probably concluded that for several reasons they could complete the road more quickly and at less cost on the hill than along the valley. First, trees were smaller on the less fertile ridge than in the more fertile valley below, and more easily felled. Second, annual flooding had deposited fine silt and clay in Karr Valley over the 10,000 years since the glaciers retreated. Water did not percolate through the densely packed soil easily, creating drainage problems in the swampy valley. Third, during the winter months, the road froze earlier, which facilitated travel, and the wind blew snow off the road to lower elevations. Fourth, higher elevation meant less road damaging erosion during heavy rainstorms and spring floods.

Agricultural productivity was higher in Karr Valley than along Turnpike Road. Karr Valley farms were consistently more valuable than Turnpike Road farms, as indicated by average price per acre for a sample of recorded transactions (Index of Deeds Part A. Allegany County). Karr Valley's bottom land Erie Series soils are more fertile than Turnpike Road's hillside Volusia soils (Personal communication, Alfred University geologist Michele Hluchy). The early Turnpike Road settlers in effect traded off poor soils for a low per acre price, ease of clearing, a south facing slope that lengthened the growing season, and access to a good road.

Many farms were well established in Karr Valley before the first permanent settlers broke ground after completion of Turnpike Road. They clearly preferred to invest their labor in clearing land and building a road in the fertile valley with a creek running through it that provided life sustaining water and power to operate a saw mill. After Turnpike Road was constructed in 1811, settlers immediately located along it, attracted by ready access to the market and the opportunities to earn income providing food and shelter to travelers along the road.

During its brief life, Turnpike Road was a major thoroughfare westward. The turnpike was one hundred feet wide, corduroyed with tree trunks in the swampier places. Streams of travelers headed west to their new lands in western New York and Ohio. Stage coaches carried mail and passengers from Bath to Angelica; at best, a stage made 40 miles a day with two changes of horses. Several houses along Turnpike Road served as inns and stables for passing travelers. Early travelers were quite uniform in their condemnation of the services provided by these inns (McNall 1952). Since inns had little competition, innkeepers had little incentive to provide value for dollars. And since few customers ever returned, the innkeeper had no need to build a good reputation. For their part, travelers no doubt behaved in unruly and inconsiderate ways. Since innkeeper and traveler would never see each other again, each player was likely to defect on the other (2, 2). Had they expected a long future together, the innkeeper would have provided better service (3) and the traveler would have improved his behavior (3).

Poor accommodation was expensive in 1840. One informant whose aunt owned a roadside inn recalled that during the 1840s, "Horses to hay, supper, lodging and breakfast cost a traveler 62 cents which included a drink of whiskey before supper and before breakfast if the guest desired it." (Local New York State Clippings, volume 10, Fillmore, Wide Awake Club Library 1874). By comparison, decent accommodation in a budget motel and a modest dinner nearby might cost $62 today, or 100 times more than the 62 cents a road-weary traveler paid in 1820. But a modestly paid worker today earns perhaps $20,000, or 200 times the $100 earned annually by the average worker in the 1820s.

Early settlement patterns in the 29 towns of Allegany County reveal that settlers in western New York did not distribute themselves randomly across the heavily forested landscape. Settlers arriving before 1825 built their homes at low elevations and in areas closer to the major market towns of Bath and Batavia. These villages in turn connected to good roads heading back east. Early settlers minimized transportation costs, following creek and river valleys, avoiding elevations and locating close to regional economic centers. They also tended to settle in the same towns as had the earliest settlers. Within towns, early migrants settled in or near villages to benefit from economies of scale. Together, neighboring settlers could provide essential social infrastructure (church and school) and physical infrastructure (sawmill, general store and improved roads).

These findings are limited to Allegany County towns, but early settlement patterns in all of western New York may be similar. Early settlers throughout western New York had the same incentive to avoid high transportation costs and to enjoy the benefits of specialization and economies of scale available in local villages.

NOTES

1. Special thanks go to Mark Michael McGovern who coauthored an earlier version of this material, Diana Sinton for her GIS data on physical characteristics of the landscape and Arthur L. Greil for his help with statistical analysis.

2. The value of Pearson's r varies between 0 (the two variables are not related) to 1 (the two variables are perfectly correlated). Given the complexity of the factors that shape human behavior, a correlation of .34 indicates a strong relationship. The nega-

tive sign means that as the independent variable increases in value, the dependent variable decreases in value. Date of initial settlement is dichotomized; towns settled before 1812 = 0, towns settled after 1816 = 1.

3. Victor Marie Dupont and Josephine Dupont lived in Angelica New York from 1806 to 1809. They corresponded extensively with family members living in Wilmington DE and New York city. The original letters are located in the Hagley Museum and Library, Wilmington DE, which is the repository of the Dupont family papers. Thomas Rasmussen and Margaret Rasmussen xeroxed some 200 pages of material on a visit to the museum in July 2001. Cecelia Beach, Professor of French at Alfred University, read the letters and enlisted the assistance of two students majoring in French, Alexis Cretekos and Jaime Ward, in translating them. The original letters were deciphered and an English translation prepared during 2002 and 2003. These documents are a valuable addition to the sparse first hand written accounts of life on the western New York frontier.

4. Path coefficients show that the lower a town's average elevation, the earlier the settlement date (.30), the larger the town population in 1840 ($-.34$), and the more likely that railroad or canal will run through it (-35). Railroad planners, like early settlers, avoided high elevations. They no doubt preferred to serve existing population centers like Angelica in 1850, but they preferred to avoid high elevations and chose the more circuitous route through Wellsville and Belmont. The closer a town is to regional commercial centers, the earlier the date of initial settlement (.22) and the larger is town population in 1840 ($-.30$), controlling for elevation.

Chapter Three

Making Farms and Raising Crops
1810–1850

Crops could be grown easily on the rich bottom lands and easy transportation facilitated trading along the Mohawk and Susquehanna River systems to the east and north of Allegany County, where the core of Iroquois civilization was located. The Seneca had a modest presence in Allegany County, with one permanent village located along the Genesee River at Caneadea and a few unfortified temporary villages. Allegany County itself is named for the *Allegwi* people, early inhabitants driven from the area by the Iroquois, and *hanna*, their word for river. The Seneca mostly passed through the county on their way to pursue trade or war with Native Americans in Pennsylvania, or to seek good fur trapping or hunting possibilities in the remote forest. Early settlers followed established Indian trails in the stream valleys. Over time, these trails evolved into permanent roads that automobiles use today.

THE COLLAPSE OF IROQUOIS POWER IN WESTERN NEW YORK

In the first half of the eighteenth century, the Iroquois had considerable influence over Pennsylvania-based and Middle Western Indian tribes. They held the balance of power in the Anglo-French struggle for control of the interior, and Europeans paid top dollar for furs largely supplied by the Iroquois (Aquila 1983, p. 235). Both parties gained by cooperating in this non-zero-sum game (3, 3). English or French gained an ally against their European enemy and both Europeans and Iroquois profited from the fur trade. The Iroquois were treated with respect so long as they held the balance of power in the New York interior and white settlers were not yet seeking access to Iroquois lands.

When French power collapsed in North America in 1763 after the French and Indian War, the Iroquois nation declined. Iroquois men no longer had the opportunity to practice diplomacy; fur trapping and hunting became less profitable; and alcohol was too readily available (Richter 1992, p. 265). The revolutionary war presented the Iroquois with one last opportunity to play their rivals, now the American colonists and the British, against each other. Some Iroquois leaders favored neutrality, others hoped to stem the tide of white settlers moving into their lands by allying with the British. In 1779, General George Washington sent General James Clinton and an army of several thousand men on an expedition to western New York to destroy Seneca villages and burn their crops. Clinton's troops soundly defeated a British and Seneca force at Newton (Elmira), and some 5,000 Senecas sought refuge with the British at Fort Niagara in Canada (Mintz 1999). After 1779, Indians posed no military threat to the stream of white settlers who poured into their lands in central and western New York (Wallace 1970, p. 141).

The Seneca were pressured to sign away their rights to the land of western New York for pennies per acre to the states of Massachusetts and New York and ultimately to land speculators who bought and sold millions of acres. European land speculators believed they were buying the right to exclusive use of the land, including the right to force the Indians to leave the land. The Indians mistakenly believed that they were allowing a few Europeans to share use of their land in customary ways.

The few settlers who lived in the central New York and Pennsylvania wilderness lived in constant fear of Indian raids. No one knew for sure whether the Indians had been cowed into submission, or if angered braves penned up at Fort Niagara, Canada would seek to recover their lost lands. Stories of Indians exacting revenge by slaughtering settlers, killing their animals and burning their houses, carrying off their women and torturing their prisoners were widely circulated. Inflicting pain on prisoners was part of Indian rituals of mourning, an expression of grief for slain family members. Settlers viewed Indian torture simply as an expression of primitive savagery. Anticipation of such consequences, however unlikely in 1806, often colored relations between local Indians and white settlers.

As relations with England deteriorated in the years prior to 1812, settlers feared that British troops would encourage their Indian allies to reclaim their historic lands by force. As one French immigrant and early resident of Angelica village, Marie D'Autremont, worried in an 1807 letter to her son in Paris, "There is talk of war. The English have captured a frigate and they say the savages of Canada want to win those of this country to join their cause. I assure you that I am far from satisfied. These gentlemen (Indians) are not polite people." Her son Alexander D'Autremont wrote, ". . . there are rumors here of war with the English and the people are afraid and fearing that the Indians will attack them. Almost all the farms are for sale." (D'Autremont Letters). Given the climate of fear and uncertainty, little new territory in Allegany County was settled between 1808 and 1816.

The Caneadea Indian reservation in Allegany County covered a two mile by eight mile area from Rossburg to Caneadea along both banks of the Genesee River. The Seneca, having developed resistance to malaria, were able to produce crops in the fertile Genesee Valley in a leisurely way. Early white settlers avoided the unhealthy river valley, preferring to clear the forests above the river valley. By 1826, they were developing immunities to swamp fever and were ready to cultivate the rich bottom lands of the Genesee. The local Seneca were pressured to sell their reservation to a land developer, and by 1830 all of the Seneca had left for the Tonawanda or Allegheny reservations. Few local settlers protested their departure.

Institutions to discuss disagreements and to constrain aggressive behavior were poorly developed. In the absence of shared social institutions, differences were settled by force, and whites had more resources—numbers, weapons, technology and legal clout—than did Indians. Legally, governments endorsed white claims to private ownership of local land, not the Indian view that land belonged to the community and individuals could make use of the land as needed. Whites also had much stronger technology at their disposal, including weapons, wagons and water wheels. Settlers appropriated traditionally Native American lands, forcing Indians to sign treaties ceding all claims to their land. In the conflict between Native Americans and whites, local whites imposed most of the acts of discrimination, physical assault and murder on the declining Indian population. Even when the Indians were much weakened, whites continued to fear them out of all proportion to the real threat they posed.

Whites were unlikely to try cooperative behavior based on negotiated compromise and mutual respect (3, 3) in these circumstances. Dominant white settlers scored better (4) by crushing their weak Native American competitors (1), banishing survivors to small reservations. Although mistrust and conflict largely defined relations between local Indians and Allegany County settlers, occasional acts of cooperation took place among white and Indian neighbors. Settlers traded bread or tools to neighboring Indians for hides and game in a live and let live spirit of coexistence (3, 3). White farmers provided bread to Indians today in exchange for the promise of venison from tomorrow's hunting expedition (Merrill, 1908 p. 73).

CREDITORS AND DEBTORS: LAND SPECULATORS
AND EARLY SETTLERS

A few large land companies held title to most western New York land. Allegany County was formed from lands owned by the Holland Land Company, the Morris Reserve and Phelps Gorham (Ellis, Frost and Fink 1964).

These original land speculators were not in a particularly strong bargaining position with respect to the prospective settlers moving west around 1800. Large tracts of land were available on the western New York frontier, and buyers could pick and choose. Philip Church, Charles Williamson and Joseph Ellicott eagerly sold off 50 or 100 acre parcels of land for about $1.50 per acre, a substantial mark up on land for which they paid pennies an acre.

With land readily available and labor in very short supply in western New York, a potential large land owner could not entice settlers to work as paid laborers or tenants on large landholdings owned by someone else. Conflict between large landowners and indebted tenant farmers had been common in the Hudson Valley during the revolutionary war period (Mark 1965). In the 1770s, the majority of small farmers in Vermont sympathized with the patriot tenant farmers in New York against the politically dominant Tory landowning elite. Their sons who migrated to western New York in the years after 1800 were strongly committed to the principle that small farmers should own their

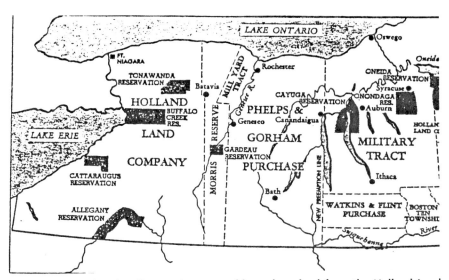

Figure 3.1.   Settlers in Allegany County could purchase land from the Holland Land Company, the Morris Reserve or Phelps Gorham (Ellis Frost and Fink (1964).

own land, not rent from large landowners. Some early settlers arrived from Pennsylvania, where in the 1790s labor was abundant, and farmers who fell behind in their land payments faced foreclosure (Bouton 2000, p. 855).

The landlord tenant system was stable when the players negotiated mutually acceptable terms. Tenants were granted secure leases, their landlords might extend credit and improve roads and landlords eased tenant obligations during hard times. In return, tenants would pay their rents in timely fashion, defer to their landlord, not support anti-rent protest movements and not emigrate westward (Huston 2000, p. 192; Summerhill 2005, p. 32). So long as each player cooperated dependably, landlord and tenant each scored well (3, 3). Of course, each player was constantly tempted to gain an advantage (4), which could lead to a retaliatory defection and a new cycle of mutually destructive behavior (2, 2). Mutual defection was common in the 1800s; by mid-century, landlords had sold off their holdings and the landlord tenant game in New York ended.

Philip Church purchased 100,000 acres of land in Allegany County's Genesee River Valley from the financially strapped Robert Morris sight unseen at a foreclosure sale in Canandaigua. To attract settlers to his lands, Church offered buyers of less than 100 acres a lower per acre price than the price he charged large land purchasers. He no doubt calculated that his future prosperity depended upon attracting labor to the western New York wilderness, so the more small holders the better.

Capital was in short supply on the frontier, and most would-be large landowners were speculators who were not bringing much cash to the transaction. Church knew that about 70 percent of Charles Williamson's mortgage defaulters had large tracts of 200 or more acres, and would walk away from large tracts bought for speculation (Silsby 1969, p. 143). He also would have been familiar with the anti-rent activism and popular protest back east where large landowners rented land to tenant farmers on exploitive terms (Humphrey 2004; Huston 2000).

Church might also have liked his chances to maintain his economic position and social prestige in the context of many small landowners. He attempted unsuccessfully to prevent newcomers from setting up stores and sawmills in competition with his own. Josephine Dupont wrote of her husband Victor's new general store, "It is a little opposition to the Church store which I don't think made the Captain happy but they can't have hoped to found a town and populate 100 thousand acres without seeing this sort of competition. However they do not like it. They told Mr. Cruger that he couldn't build any mills - not even a saw mill" (W3-4953 February 2, 1808).

Land speculators provided several valuable services to entice settlers to migrate to western New York. First, company surveyors divided western New

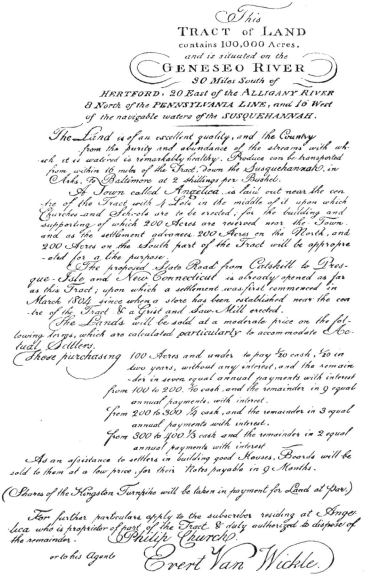

This

TRACT of LAND

contains 100,000 Acres,

and is situated on the

GENESEO RIVER

90 Miles South of

HERTFORD, 20 East of the ALLIGANY RIVER
8 North of the PENNSYLVANIA LINE, and 16 West
of the navigable waters of the SUSQUEHANNAH.

The Land is of an excellent quality, and the Country from the purity and abundance of the streams with which it is watered is remarkably healthy. Produce can be transported from within 16 miles of the Tract, down the Susquehannah, in Arks, to Baltimore at 2 shillings per Bushel.

A Town called Angelica, is laid out near the centre of the Tract with 4 Lots in the middle of it upon which Churches and Schools are to be erected; for the building and supporting of which 200 Acres are reserved near the Town, and as the settlement advances, 200 Acres on the North, and 200 Acres on the South part of the Tract will be appropriated for a like purpose.

The proposed State Road from Catskill to Presque-Isle and New Connecticut is already opened as far as this Tract; upon which a settlement was first commenced in March 1804, since when a store has been established near the centre of the Tract & a Grist and Saw-Mill erected.

The Lands will be sold at a moderate price on the following Terms, which are calculated particularly to accommodate Actual Settlers.

Those purchasing 100 Acres and under to pay £20 cash, £20 in two years, without any interest, and the remainder in seven equal annual payments with interest.

from 100 to 200. ⅖ cash, and the remainder in 9 equal annual payments, with interest.

from 200 to 300 ½ cash, and the remainder in 3 equal annual payments with interest.

from 300 to 400. ⅓ cash and the remainder in 2 equal annual payments with interest.

As an assistance to settlers in building good Houses, Boards will be sold to them at a low price, for their Notes payable in 9 Months.

(Shares of the Kingston Turnpike will be taken in payment for Land at par.)

For further particulars apply to the subscriber residing at Angelica who is proprietor of part of the Tract & duly authorized to dispose of the remainder. *Philip Church.*

or to his Agent *Evert Van Wickle.*

Figure 3.2. Philip Church sought buyers for his land near the village of Angelica. Church's central village square, water supply, churches on each corner and early nineteenth century buildings grace the village of Angelica today. Church's pricing policy encouraged small holders to buy less than 100 acres. It discouraged potential large landholders who might compete with him.

York into towns, sections and lots to facilitate the transfer of land to buyers of small holdings. Allegany County is divided into 29 towns, each as close to six square miles as possible. Each town was subdivided into 16 sections, each containing about 315 acres. Then each section was subdivided into 12 lots of about 26 acres, as Figure 3.3 illustrates.

Lots were rectangular in shape with the narrow end facing road and stream. Nearly all settlers built their homes on the road and farmed their fields up the hillside. The goal was to make all lots desirable to buyers. Holland surveyor and land agent Joseph Ellicott intended to "make each lot equally convenient to water and to distribute rich alluvial soil among more settlers and to avoid leaving the company with the backlands." Where terrain permitted, roads were built along town lines.

Second, land speculators bore the costs of retailing land to westward bound settlers. Land speculators sold the land they purchased in the late eighteenth century quickly, making a profit as land value increased. Phelps and Gorham acquired 2.5 million acres east of the Genesee River from the Seneca at Big Tree in 1788 at three cents per acre. They doubled their money when they sold the land to Robert Morris for eight cents an acre in 1790. A year later, Morris sold the land to the Pulteney group for 26 cents an acre. Morris sold another chunk of 3.3 million acres to the Dutch-owned Holland Land Company for 33 cents per acre (Chazanoff 1979).

Third, land speculators also built essential infrastructure that eased the burden for settlers moving into the forested wilderness. The Holland Land Company subsidized road construction, provided tavern owners with operating subsidies and gave discounts to land purchasers who would attract future buyers (Wyckoff). Charles Williamson, the Pulteney land agent, sought to attract settlers by building roads and laying out towns. Borrowers were offered low interest rates, a small down payment, and six to ten years to repay their loan. But he could not charge prices high enough to recover the company's investment, and his successor Joseph Ellicott favored a policy of no frills and rock bottom prices to attract settlers (Brooks 1996).

A sample of 12 Karr Valley property transactions from 1810-1818 in the town of Almond reveals that land typically sold for $2 per acre. Some land sold for as little as $1 per acre or as much as $2.50 per acre, depending upon land quality, proximity to road and creek, and number of acres purchased. Labor was in short supply on the frontier, and land companies were eager to attract new settlers.

Tension existed between large landholders and small banks on the one hand and hard-pressed indebted farmers on the other. In the game between creditors and debtors, creditors were not in a particularly strong position. They

Figure 3.3.   This map for the town of Almond illustrates the surveyor's work that has provided the framework for land sales for 200 years. Early settlement depended upon good legal title to the land and access to road and stream. Karr Valley Road runs in an east west direction along the Karr Valley creek. Turnpike Road runs parallel to Karr Valley Road to the south on top of a ridge. Today, interstate Route 86 runs between the two historic roads.

Source: Samuel Beers, Atlas of Allegany County

could threaten to foreclose, but at auction the land would not fetch the sum owed, and many debtors could easily walk away from the area. Village shop-keepers had to extend credit to cashless customers and to accept payment in ashes, hides or whiskey. One shopkeeper placed humorous ads in the local newspaper chiding his delinquent debtors (Silsby 1969, p. 155). At best, in the Prisoner's Dilemma game, creditors made concessions to debtors, who in turn made a good faith effort to make regular payments on their debt (3, 3). Given the harsh economic conditions on the frontier, that was the best out-come available to the players. If relations between creditor and debtor took the form of continuous low-grade hostility, the creditor harassing the debtor and the debtor hiding his assets to avoid making payments, the players do less well in the game (2, 2).

Creditors had some advantages in the game played with settler debtors. Early settlers judged the agricultural potential of land by the nature of the for-est cover, and the land companies provided the information. For the land sur-veyors of the Holland Land Company, type of tree cover influenced their val-uation of the agricultural potential of a land section. Sugar maple, elm, hickory, black cherry and basswood indicated good agricultural potential. Beech also grew in promising soil, but their spreading root system was hard to clear. Ash, tamarack and cedar grew in poorly drained, nutrient deficient soils, and lands with large concentrations of spruce, fir and hemlock were as-sociated with colder clay soils and a short growing season. Their judgments based on long experience are confirmed by agronomists today who do chem-ical analysis of soil in their laboratories (Wyckoff 1981). Of course, some set-tlers were disappointed with the quality of the land they purchased when in-experienced surveyors misidentified trees or exaggerated the presence of trees associated with more fertile lands.

But indebted settlers were slow to make payments to the land companies. Settlers believed that any increase in value was due to their work, not the company's land; that one should meet obligations to neighbors before mak-ing payments to the land company; and that as a matter of justice the land company should not press for payments due during times of hardship (Brooks 1996). Settlers typically paid off their debts to neighbors and village mer-chants first, or loaned money to neighbors at higher interest rates than the land company was charging them (McNall 1952). Creditors had reason to fear reprisal if they pressed their debtors too hard. More subtly, debtors made fun of creditors and admired debtors who successfully escaped the claims of their creditors (Silsby 1969, p. 158).

Cash poor settlers were sometimes allowed to make payments to the com-pany in labor, building roads. The land companies wanted settlers to invest their labor in improving the land by clearing rocks, weeding fields, and building fences. But settlers were better served by abandoning fields after a few years and using their scarce labor to clear new fields. Abandoned fields reverted to second growth brush, which was difficult to clear and therefore less valuable to the company should the settler fail to make payments on his debt (Brooks 1996).

A constant concern for the land companies was that settlers would poach old growth prime timber on neighboring company land. The Holland Land Company employed informers to report on illegal cutting of timber on company lands. Seth Wetmore, an Allegany County informer in 1825, reported that "Two brothers named Young cut three pine trees, drawed the logs to the mill and applied the boards on the School House" and that "Elijah Hyde cut two green pines and two that was down. Sawed and made use of them to cover his buildings." (Brooks 1996, p. 93). Informants received a cash payment or forgiveness of money owed to the company for each trespasser who made restitution.

The conflicting interest of creditors and debtors was a staple of local politics in the 1820s. A convention of settlers from 27 Allegany and Steuben towns met in Bath in January 1830 to protest the policies of Pulteney estate agents. These assembled debtors objected that Pulteney agents insisted that debtors make annual payments on their debt and that Pulteney compounded the interest on unpaid debt in subsequent years. Robert Troup, the Pulteney agent, adopted a conciliatory tone but insisted that borrowers make payments on their debts. Troup noted that the Pulteney Estate promoted the welfare of the settlers by building roads, subsidizing construction of churches and schools, and recruiting blacksmiths and other craftsmen to settle in local villages. He agreed to reduce debt where an appraisal, done by local farmers mutually acceptable to the petitioner and to Troup, indicated that the lands were overvalued. This concession addressed an important problem. Many early settlers signed contracts without having a detailed understanding of the quality of their land. Available site descriptions were provided by the company employed surveyors whose incentive was to over estimate the land's agricultural potential. Troup also guaranteed a fair price for each bushel of wheat and head of cattle offered for sale in Bath.

Local protesters did not accept Troup's response. They pledged to petition the legislature for relief and to suspend all payments to the Pulteney agency. Troup was adamant. He complained that the settlers had come voluntarily and purchased their farms at the prices commonly asked by landholders at the time and after having explored the lots to judge correctly the value of their lands. Recent purchasers saddled with heavy debt relative to the income generating potential of their lands were more deserving, thought Troup. He instructed his agents to reduce annual payments on a case by case basis, and to take legal action against farmers who failed to make payments on their debt (Mau 1958).

The first murder in Allegany County involved a land foreclosure case. A debtor, David Howe, was hanged in 1824 for murdering Othello Church, who held the mortgage on Howe's land. The murderer had much public support. As the incident was later reported, "Howe's creditors seized his grain and when the luckless debtor entreated them to spare enough for next spring's crops, they only laughed in his face. And when driven to the verge of desperation by seeing the bread that ought to go into his children's mouths vanish into the insatiable maws of his persecuting Shylock-like creditors, he approached Church, who not content with ravaging the grain fields began to carry off the garden vegetables. Howe in vain implored him to leave some food for his little children" (Allegany County Republican, November 25, 1881. *Local New York State Clippings*[1]).

Land company agents were vigilant in their efforts to collect money that local farmers owed. McNall reports that of 583 mortgages recorded in Allegany County, only 13 ended in foreclosures. But the large land companies found it expensive to exact payments from local farmers, and they sold mortgages to local owners and speculators in large numbers (McNall 1952, p. 226).

Settlers faced several problems in the 1820s, and many walked away from their newly cleared holdings. Construction of the Erie Canal reduced the value of Susquehanna River basin lands in the Allegany County towns of Almond and Alfred. Agricultural prices slumped as European agricultural production revived following the Napoleonic wars. Opening up more fertile western lands in Ohio at $1.25 per acre slowed the rise in value of Allegany and Steuben County lands.

CARVING A FARM IN THE WILDERNESS

When settlers walked into Allegany County in the first years of the nineteenth century, they perceived the heavily forested landscape as a place to be feared and an enemy to be conquered. The first settlers moved into the heavily forested Allegany County wilderness in the years after 1796, making the first permanent settlements in the Susquehanna River valley towns of Almond and Andover. Several Pennsylvania men cleared a few acres of land in Almond, built 20 x 26 foot log cabins, planted wheat in the summer of 1796, then returned to Pennsylvania to collect their families and return in the spring of 1797. The settler triumphant over the dark forces of nature is well conveyed in Figure 3.4. After the settler's hard fought struggle against the forest, the dark forces of nature surround the cabin that occupies the center of the scene.

Trees were a formidable opponent for settlers seeking to transform dark forest to sunny field. Removing trees typically required five to eight years of hard work (Whitney 1994). Widening paths through the forest to accommodate a wagon was exhausting work. And the forest was the menacing home of wolves, opportunistic predators picking off slow moving and defenseless farm animals that were the farmer's most valuable asset. *Allegany and Its People* is filled with old timer's reminiscences about moments of personal danger, and bounties on livestock-destroying predators whose bone-chilling howls filled the night (Minard 1896). A poem by early Allegany County resident Alfred B. Street captures the heroic struggle of the early settler against the forces of darkness and danger of the forest.

> Through the deep wilderness, where scarce the sun
> Can cast his darts along the winding path
> The Pioneer is Treading; in his grasp
> Is his keen axe, that wondrous instrument,
> That, like the talisman, transforms
> Deserts into fields and cities. He has left
> The Home in which his early years were past,
> And led by hope, and full of restless strength
> Has plunged within the forest, there to plant
> His destiny. Beside some rapid stream,
> He rears his log-built cabin. When the chains
> On winter fetter nature, and no sound
> Disturbs the echoes of the dreary woods,
> Saved when some stem cracks sharply with the frost,
> Then merrily rings his axe, and tree on tree
> Crashes to earth; and when the long keen night
> Mantles the wilderness in solemn gloom,
> He sits beside his ruddy hearth, and hears
> The fierce wolf snarling at the cabin door,
> Or through the lowly casement sees his eye
> Gleam like a burning coal.
> Source: Minard 1896, p. 45.

After the initial wave of settlers from Pennsylvania, most settlers who followed in large numbers in the next two decades came to Allegany County from New England. The New England farm supported a family in relative comfort, land prices were high there, and those who could afford to stay did so. Why did some New Englanders choose to migrate?

First, population growth pressured the New England farm family. It made no sense to subdivide the land among several children, since postage stamp size mini farms could not support a family. If a farm family had two or three

Figure 3.4.   This engraving by Artist Ebenezer Mix depicts the process of settlement in western New York (Mau 1944). Cabin and spring house occupy the center of the clearing. A hide on the side wall of the cabin is being cured. The owner is clearing the land, cutting a felled tree into lengths. Two oxen will haul the logs to the nearest sawmill. In the spring, crops will be planted among the tree stumps. This frontier family also has a cow and three sheep.

adult sons age 20 to 30 and the head of household was in his 50s, the farm was usually taken over by whichever son could operate the farm well and who would provide care for the aging parents. Other sons were given financial assistance to buy neighboring land, or to migrate westward to the frontier. In 1800, prices for marginal land in New England and Pennsylvania exceeded $20 per acre, while forested land on the frontier could be had for $2 per acre. Daughters sought a marriage partner on a neighboring farm or in the village. An established farm owner who lost his wife was able to find a younger replacement quickly. Gravestones in old western New York cemeteries provide many examples.

Second, farms in New England were costly, and migration was an attractive option for young individuals and families who were cash poor but muscle rich. After investing years of hard work, they would still have years to enjoy the fruits of their labors (Shaw 1975, p.18). Migration also appealed to those who by temperament were risk takers. And migrants who were dissatisfied with their position in the local community– social failures in the community and family black sheep-might try their luck on the frontier (Davis 1977). Groups of relatives or neighbors, sometimes members of dissident religious communities like the Seventh Day Baptists, moved to the same western New York towns.

How much did it cost the early settler to move to the western New York frontier from New England, to clear the land, build a cabin and begin growing crops? Both capital and labor were in short supply on the frontier. Writing in 1806, Mrs. D'Autremont complained to her son, "One cannot find laborers as one wishes, and they cost a great deal because they are going to build a turnpike and Mr. Church engages all those he can lay his hand on. He pays them sixteen dollars per month and feeds them.." (Mrs. d'Autremont to Louis Paul, May 5, 1806, p. 20). Table 3.1 offers a rough estimate of these essential costs.

Settlers in Allegany County were heavily engaged in clearing the forest for 50 to 75 years after initial settlement about 1800. They chose one of two methods to clear the land. One method was to clear cut an acre and burn the felled trees. Forest burning cleared the land for planting, and the ashes were used to produce potash, the settler's principal source of cash. Victor Dupont offers a rare, first hand description of the forest burning process. "We have been here two days in a true hell. The weather has been so dry that everyone is burning their land and the fire has spread to their wood in several places. We are only breathing smoke and the sun is obscure and hidden. Everyone keeps watch at night to save their houses. All the fences in the town burned yesterday and the mill came close. As for me, I am no longer in danger, my own fires having spread to our neighbors" (W3-665, May 6, 1806).

A second approach to clearing the land was girdling, or removing a wide circle of bark from each tree which cut off the flow of water and nutrients from roots to leaves. The leaves withered immediately and the settler then planted crops around the dying tree, which eventually was felled and burned. However, falling limbs posed a threat to grazing animals, damaged fences and

Table 3.1. Per Family Costs of Settling the Western New York Frontier, First Six Months

Land Purchase (40 acres x $2)	$80
Migration expenses (repairs, accommodations, food)	
($1 per day x 1month)	$30
Capital equipment	$120
Yoke of oxen	$70
Ox cart	$30
Tools (hoe, axe, saw, plow)	$20
Initial land clearing, cabin construction ($1 per day × 4 months) $120	
Total	$350

Source: Gates (1960) for capital equipment estimates. The $1 per day estimate is based on the value of a day's labor in 1820. The actual expenditures of a migrant to Western New York would of course vary considerably. Collecting the resources needed to migrate would require about a year's work for the early nineteenth century farmer.

had to be cleaned up regularly. In a subsequent winter, the farmer removed the stumps.

Settlers downed trees ruthlessly, and about 12 per cent of total farm labor in Allegany County was dedicated to clearing the land (Primack 1962). As one landowner living in Europe wrote to his relative in Angelica, "I recommend that you clear up with taste and symmetry, so that my farm may have an aspect a little less wild than is generally the case in the woods. . . From the manner in which Americans clear, one would think they had a hatred of trees" (Louis Paul d'Autremont to his mother, February 3, 1806). In a setting where land was plentiful and labor scarce, devoting labor to clearing more land rather than using advanced, labor intensive farming practices to earn higher yields per acre made sound economic sense. For the settler, the initial investment of clear cutting and burning a forested acre was similar to the total cost of girdling trees over a 15-year period (Whitney 1994).

Unusually cold weather in 1816 intensified the hardships endured by the first settlers. Intense volcanic activity in Southeast Asia in 1815 cast sulfur and soot particles in to the upper atmosphere. The layer circled the globe, reducing the amount of solar energy reaching the earth (Stommel and Stommel 1979). In Allegany County, winter snow covered the ground through mid April, spring snow covered the ground in May, and a sharp freeze ended the growing season early in September. Settlers long remembered the year with no summer.

American farmers on the frontier tended to cultivate large fields poorly rather than small fields intensively, contrary to practice in Europe where land was scarce and labor and capital more plentiful. Because the first generation of Allegany County settlers devoted more scarce labor to clearing land than to manuring fields, caring for cattle, weeding, or alternating crops to preserve soil fertility, they are best described as farm makers rather than farmers (Whitney 1994). The Holland Land Company contemptuously referred to these farm makers as transient wood choppers (Brooks 1996). Advanced agricultural techniques that were well established in England where land was valued at $20 per acre were inappropriate on the frontier where land was cheap. Yields per acre on the early nineteenth century Allegany County farm were less than half those of an English farm of the day.

Settlers who expected to clear their land purchased at $2 per acre, then sell it for $10 per acre and move west to begin again the process of land clearing had no incentive to invest capital in improved agricultural techniques. Their small collection of cattle and other animals could not produce enough dung to fertilize their available acres. Clover, apples and root crops were not widely used as food supplements for their livestock. Selective breeding was practically unknown for both technical and philosophical reasons. Farmers committed to democratic, egalitarian values wanted no royal breeding stock contaminating their cattle (McMurry 1995). Farm makers busily clearing their land did not care for their animals in the early decades. Years passed before the farmer built a barn; men were known to get up during wintry nights to chase their cows around so they would not freeze (Merrill 1908).

The hated trees that absorbed years of heavy labor and harbored threatening wolves also were a valuable resource in the early subsistence economy. Trees were shaped into logs and fashioned into the log cabin, the settler's first home. A log cabin required about 80 logs plus shingle for the roof (Whitney 1994). Log cabins were drafty since logs shifted and shrank as they dried. They were dark, since creating window openings was hard work and made the settler's family more vulnerable to the forces of nature. And log cabins were small, because heavy logs could not easily be lifted to build a second story for sleeping rooms, and weak foundations did not support weighty logs dependably. These drafty, small homes were quickly replaced by sawn lumber houses. White pine was preferred for construction, being strong, light weight, and easily worked into boards, planks and shingles.

The fireplace in the log cabin consumed large amounts of wood for heating and cooking. Cast iron wood stoves which dramatically increased wood burning efficiency were not available until mid-century (Adams 2000). The forest also provided fencing to keep domestic animals from wandering off or finding morsels in the family garden plot and to keep wolves and other forest predators away from the family's chicken and sheep. The post and rail fence required much labor to dig post holes and fit the rails to the posts. Furthermore, the fence required considerable maintenance as the underground posts would rot in a few short years. The Virginia rail or zigzag fence required more wood but less labor, and therefore was preferred on the Allegany frontier where wood was abundant and labor scarce. To fence an acre, the settler needed about 800 four-inch diameter rails, each 10 feet long.

Firewood and fencing material of a desirable size was readily available because hardwoods tend to devote the carbohydrate reserves stored in their root systems to spreading new shoots from their cut stumps. The sprouts from a hardwood stump would be ready to harvest for firewood or fence rails in 10 or 20 years. Among the more vigorous sprouters were black walnut, chestnut, hickory and white oak.

Production of potash was the most attractive source of income for the early settler. Potash was the most important industrial chemical in 1810, being used in the production of glass, soap and gunpowder. To produce it, the settler ran water through hard wood ashes to leach out potassium carbonate and other salts. After boiling off the water, the remaining lye was heated in a kettle to burn off impurities, leaving pure potash. White estimates that about 30 percent of the area in Allegany County cleared from 1834 to 1845 was used for the production of potash, and the value of potash production was about $5 per acre (P.L. White 1979). Some farmers carried the potash to the general store in the neighboring village. Others traded with ash gatherers who picked their way over Allegany County roads exchanging cloth, sewing materials coffee and hardware for the farmers' ashes.

Trees had other economic uses. Tannin extracted from the bark of hemlock was used in tanning, the process of converting raw animal hides into flexible, water-resistant leather. Early settlers boiled the spring time flow of sap from sugar maple trees to produce maple sugar for home consumption and for barter at the general store in the nearby village. Mrs. d'Autremont complained to her son in 1806 that "there are no maple trees on our land which I resent because sugar is a great treat" (Marie d'Autremont to Louis Paul d'Autremont, p. 19). But maple sugar production was never a central activity in the western New York frontier. By 1820, cane sugar production was well established in Louisiana and available at low cost in northern markets. The New York State 1855 census indicates that maple sugar production contributed modestly to the Allegany County farm economy.

STANDARD OF LIVING IN THE FRONTIER CABIN

Life on the frontier involved much hard work and material consumption was limited to essentials. The daily diet of the frontier settler was simple and scant, featuring wheat, corn, buckwheat, oats, peas and potatoes. Marie d'Autremont, the wife of a royalist executed during the French Revolution, migrated to America with her two sons in 1806 and purchased 200 acres of land from Phillip Church in Angelica. Her letters to another son, Louis Paul, provide evidence about diet on the frontier in 1806.[2] The d'Autremonts were better off than most settlers, being personal friends of the Phillip Church family and occasionally receiving funds from her son in France. She writes that supplements to the family diet included

- about three quarters lb of butter per week
- "coffee" made of roasted corn, along with one lb of real coffee per year
- tea from locally harvested mint
- about 26 hens in the year
- three pigs

(Marie D'Autremont to Louis Paul d'Autremont, September 1, 1807).

Settlers also converted grain to whiskey on the frontier. Josephine Dupont remarked, "Victor is proudly selling by the quart the barrels of whiskey he gets in exchange for the gunpowder." (W3-4940 March 21 1807).

Goods available at the general store were prohibitively expensive. A pound of coffee, for example, cost 40 cents, a pound of nails 16 cents and a pair of gloves 75 cents (Gates 1960.) Victor Dupont reported that best selling items at his newly opened store included wine, muslin cloth, pottery and glassware, hardware and chewing tobacco (W3-701, July 25, 1808). The subsistence farm family perhaps generated about $50 per year in cash sales. Marie D'Autremont reports that in Angelica, "The stores do not barter for grain. One must pay with money" (Letter to Louis Paul D'Autremont, September 1 1807). If the frontier farm family could not produce an item themselves, they often went without it.

Deer were an important but uncertain supplement to the household food supply. Indians sold venison to settlers for "next to nothing" (Victor Dupont to Eleuthiere Dupont, W3-691, January 7 1807). Guns manufactured 200 years ago varied in quality and accuracy, and success in hunting deer required luck and great skill. Many young men had neither the patience nor the skill to hunt successfully, and farm families preferred to raise their own domestic meat supply than to depend upon the uncertainties of hunting. Certainly skilled hunters who understood the habits of game animals, owned a good gun, and possessed excellent eyesight and steady nerves sometimes bartered venison with neighbors in exchange for their work on the hunter's farm or food from a neighbor's kitchen. But when the local store keeper paid one pound of tea for one deer delivered to the store, the deer hunter had no incentive to specialize. Better to hunt to meet the needs of his family and perhaps his neighbors and devote extra time to clearing his land and raising crops. One Rushford resident writes, "Deer were plentiful but some men were not good hunters. David Vaughn was a mighty hunter, and often neighbors would get him to go hunting for them; all he asked was that they work on his farm while he hunted" (Merrill 1908, p. 73).

Susan Greene's survey of early nineteenth century wills suggests that when households dissolved, many no longer included a gun. Presumably, the energy, eyesight and coordination required to hunt deer successfully diminished as men grew older, and they passed their gun on to younger relatives or neighbors Greene studied 45 inventories of belongings contained in court records from 1808-1829 of folks who died without wills. She concluded that possession of looms and rifles was the exception rather than the rule on the frontier (Greene n.d.). Josephine Dupont, no stranger to privilege, said that everyone dressed simply on the frontier. "Worrying about appearances seems a joke here in Angelica. What good would it do one to display frivolous pretty things"(W3-4947 May 7 1807).

Table 3.2.   Household Textile Manufactures in Allegany County, 1825–1855

Year	Total Yards, Textiles	Population	Yards Per Capita
1825	170,415	18,164	9.38
1835	220,047	35,214	6.25
1845	213,982	40,084	5.34
1855	30,963	42,910	0.72

Source: Tryon 1917, p. 305.

Feeding grain to their animals was a convenient way to store food, providing insurance against crop failure and a welcome change in diet. In 1821, Allegany County farmers were estimated to own over 11,000 cattle, 1300 horses and 15,000 sheep (Spafford 1981). Assuming that about 18,000 people lived in Allegany County and that each household sheltered about five persons, the reported 11,000 cattle were divided among about 3600 households, or on average three cattle per household. Most frontier families owned a yoke of oxen and perhaps a milk cow.

The 15,000 sheep reveal the continuing importance of spinning and weaving wool in 1821. Eli Whitney had invented the cotton gin in 1793 to remove the seeds from short fiber cotton, giving a decisive advantage to cotton over wool. But cotton does not grow in western New York, and transportation costs to import it were prohibitive in 1821. That's why Allegany County farms had 15,000 sheep in 1821. By 1830, state of the art textile production at New England mills had driven down the price of cotton cloth from 42 cents to seven cents per yard (Tryon 1917, p. 275), and the new Erie Canal dramatically lowered transportation costs to Rochester and Buffalo. The arduous use of the spinning wheel and loom in the home was largely abandoned by 1855, as Table 3.2 indicates, and sheep largely disappeared from the Allegany County farm.

Until 1837, rising land prices encouraged farm makers to clear land, sell it to new migrants, purchase uncleared land on the westward-moving frontier and begin the process of clearing land once again. The Panic of 1837 changed the incentives for farmers. Now unable to sell their land at a profit, farmers concluded that the value of land was not in its resale value but in the value of the crops they could grow and sell. Successful farmers after 1837 thought more about how to increase yields per acre (Parkerson 1995).

BEGINNINGS OF THE DAIRY INDUSTRY

Allegany County farmers began to move from lumbering and subsistence agriculture to dairy in the 1840s, converting the denuded hills into pasture and fields for raising cattle feed. They initially had planted wheat among the rotting stumps for household use, but the short growing season in upland Allegany County doomed commercial wheat production. The mean July temperature in Allegany County is three to six degrees cooler than in lower elevation Genesee Valley counties to the north. And the cost of transportation to the Rochester High Falls milling center was higher for Allegany County farmers than for their competitors in the lower Genesee counties. Allegany County farmers never competed effectively with other New York farmers in the production of wheat. By the 1840s, wheat production in New York was under pressure from declining yields per acre, the ravages of insect pests, and the rapid expansion of wheat cultivation in the Great Lakes states (Lampard 1963).

Cows about 1840 typically produced milk from May to November, and cheese making was a seasonal activity. Counties like Allegany that are located far from urban centers commonly produced cheese, which is slow to spoil compared to whole milk. Most cheese was retained on the farm for family use, but the cheese maker traded any surplus at the general store or sold it to buyers at the farm gate. Cheese had the advantage of being a high value low bulk product. A wagon load of cheese carried four times the value of the same wagon laden with bushels of wheat, a critical factor in an era when primitive roads elevated transportation costs (Stamm 1991).

Following 75 years of dairy farming, 1875-1950, the land gradually reverted to forest as farms were abandoned after 1950. Onondaga County, located along the Erie Canal and having richer soils and higher mean temperatures, attracted settlers earlier and these settlers cleared more land and abandoned fewer acres than did Allegany County farmers (Whitney 1994, p. 152).

CONFLICT AND COOPERATION:
GAMES AMONG NEIGHBORS

The Prisoner's Dilemma game explores the consequences of one player defecting or cooperating with another player in various social settings. A player who defects pursues ones own self interest without any regard for the interest of another player, who might be a family member, a neighbor or a stranger. The second player is likely to respond by defecting, and both players score poorly (2,2). If two players refrain from selfishly defecting for short term gain and develop a habit of cooperation, each is better off (3,3).

How can people promote trust and cooperation? If people interact with each other frequently, they can signal to each other, "I know that if I do something nice for you, you are likely to return the favor." This assurance is possible only if people have a long future together. On the frontier, families and close neighbors who interact with each other regularly were more likely to cooperate, while they regarded strangers with suspicion.

The most important games on the frontier no doubt occurred within the cabin. In the self sufficient frontier household, providing for the family's essential needs was labor intensive; men and women were equally important in producing the household's subsistence requirements. Of course, in a patriarchal society, the social status of women did not match their economic importance (Ryan 1975, p. 30).

As in the New England Puritan tradition that God presided over the world, so the father presided over the frontier household. The father's responsibility was to protect his wife and children, both from outside invaders and from the temptations of sin. The bargaining position of females was weak in the context of eighteenth century patriarchal values, but for several reasons females enjoyed a stronger position on the early nineteenth century frontier. First, the new liberal ideology emphasized the rights of the individual to pursue ones own self interest and to follow one's own conscience. Women enjoyed a greater degree of freedom. Historians note, for example, the declining parental influence over the timing of their daughter's marriage and their choice of partners (Cherlin 1996). Second, the fact that women were in short supply enhanced their bargaining position within the household. Men whose wives died sought to remarry quickly, and women could choose among suitors.

To say that patriarchal culture prevailed on the frontier does not provide an adequate appreciation of the range of behaviors for males and females within any given household. Some men insisted on complete control of family resources and demanded complete subordination of women and children. In this Prisoner's Dilemma game, a tyrannical patriarch could dominate a submissive wife who cooperated rather than flee to relatives or seek the protection of another man. He had his way (4) while she suffered in silence (1). Women did have resources at their disposal; men outnumbered women on the frontier, and women readily left an unsatisfactory situation (Ryan 1981, p. 21). Women organized many neighborhood activities, and community obligations provided leverage in discussions with her patriarchal husband over how family resources should be used (Neth 1955, p. 44). A feistier wife might retaliate against her domineering husband by being a dour companion, cooking badly and defecting every day in small ways. In this perpetual low grade conflict, husband and wife each receive (2).

Other men were willing to negotiate family relationships, believing that his wife would reciprocate his cooperative behavior and contribute more to the farm's success (Neth 1995, p. 39). In this case, husband and wife each receive a score of (3). While patriarchal culture gave power and authority to the male, the male was obligated to care for and promote the well being of family members (Denhom 2006).

To consider one example of family relations on the patriarchal frontier, all of the adults in Alexandre d'Autremont's household considered Alexandre's wife to be a selfish, manipulative person. Alexandre's mother writes to her son in Paris, "Your brother is very unhappy with her but he hardly dares speak to her and when he is present during our differences, he always tells me to keep my mouth shut. . . She is very sulky. He then goes and fondles her" (Mrs. d'Autremont to Louis Paul, March 13, 1806, p. 9). Since his wife defected constantly, a positive relationship based on mutual cooperation (3,3) was not available to Alexandre and his wife. Alexandre's choices were to comply meekly (1) and allow his wife to get her way (4) or to fight back and limit his wife's gains (2,2).

Complaints about Alexandre's wife fill Mrs. d'Autremont's letters to her son in Paris and by March 1807 she had arranged to move in with the Victor Duponts in Angelica. She writes, "I think moving to town will spite that creature (Alexandre's wife) to see me in a pretty house because her main fault is jealousy, as she wants to be the master of everything. . . Alexandre had spoken to Mr. Dupont about placing Adeline (daughter of Alexandre and his wife) at their home so she could go to school. When Alexandre told his wife that he intended to give me the child, she had the impertinence to tell me that she would permit it only if I would give her everything I own. My response was that she could keep the child, that I would not make any bargain and I intended to remain master of what little I possess" (Mrs. d'Autremont to Louis Paul, September 1807, p. 63).

Mademoiselle Dohet, Alexandre's aunt, also did not get along well with Alexandre's wife. In response to her complaints, Louis Paul writes, "It appears that my sister-in-law is a little turbulent, but my dear aunt, I ask you as a good friend to make allowance for the neglected education of a young girl brought up in the woods. She does not possess the quality of gentleness, and those who have been better educated must set her an example. . . . Do not put a false susceptibility on a thousand little things that one can overlook" (Louis Paul d'Autremont to Mademoiselle Dohet, July 29, 1807 LP 83).

Louis Paul recommends here that his aunt yield quietly (1) and allow Alexandre's wife to have her way (4). He hopes that Alexandre's wife will learn to cooperate from the example of other family members. But why should Alexandre's wife settle for (3) if other family members allow her to have her way and score (4)? If family members scold, shun or refuse to allow Alexandre's wife to have her way (2, 2) she is more likely to conclude that cooperating might be a better strategy (3, 3) than defecting (2, 2).

On the frontier, settlers had reason to mistrust the intentions of strangers with whom they came in contact and defecting behavior was the result. Allegany

County's population grew rapidly during the 1820s and 1830s, and building the habit of cooperation among newcomers takes time and repeated experience. Few community institutions defined and enforced rules of cooperation. Men exceeded women in number, and some men were glad to escape confining social rules back east. More folks gathered on Saturday night in the tavern than on Sunday morning in the church (Finke and Stark 1992, p. 32)

Settled farmers and towns people also regarded itinerant hunters with suspicion as drunkards and thieves (Williams 2002). The frontier tradition of extending hospitality to passersby may be seen simply as generosity to someone in need or pleasure in conversations with someone who had information about the outside world beyond the clearing. But it may also involve not making an enemy unnecessarily. If a passerby in need of food and shelter is driven away, what was to prevent him from retaliating by stealing a chicken, knocking over a fence or worse?

Victor Dupont offered the opinion that "although the inhabitants of New York State are renowned for their good breeding, I believe that as for drinking, swearing, gambling and quarreling, Virginia and even Kentucky are no match for them" (*Journal of My Travels to the Genesee,* March 17, 1806). A year and a half later he wrote, "The race of woodsmen who start all settlements is the worst you can imagine. It isn't until they leave you to go further and sell their improvements to honest settlers that a settlement begins to prosper" (W3-697 September 1, 1807).

Permanent neighbors had reason to defect on each other too. The village of Friendship was originally known as Fighting Corners because people in the hills and people in the valley frequently engaged in personal combat, "being constantly at odds on various subjects" (*History of Friendship 1815–1865,* 1965). In 1815, the name Friendship often stated an aspiration, not a reality. Men came to blows when one man's behavior unfairly affected a neighbor's well being. A man might not show up to help his neighbors to repair the local road. His unfenced cattle might wander into a neighbor's vegetable garden. Or he might not cut thistles to prevent their seeds from blowing into a neighbor's field.

Local county and town governments passed laws requiring people to cooperate with their neighbors. The town of Friendship required in 1815 that owners of cattle keep their cattle out of their neighbor's fields. In 1822, they required farmers to cut thistles to prevent seed dispersal in their neighbors' lands. Men were required to work on local road maintenance projects annually ((*History of Friendship 1815–1965*). These laws indicate the limits of social approval and disapproval in promoting cooperative behavior in the community.

Consider the cattle fencing problem. If two neighbors take the trouble to fence in their cattle, their own vegetable gardens are secure (3, 3). If one neighbor cooperates by building his fence while his neighbor doesn't, the co-operator loses out. He has worked hard on the fence, and his vegetables are still eaten by his neighbor's animals (1). His defecting neighbor has not spent his time and energy to pen his cattle, and he has a good crop of vegetables (4). If neither neighbor fences his cattle, they both share their vegetables with the cattle (2, 2).

Settlers on the Western New York frontier sought ways to facilitate coop-erative values and behavior by promoting a long future together. One way to promote cooperative, trusting behavior was for several households to move to the frontier together, sharing established bonds based on family or religion (Parkerson 1995). From day one, the newcomers were confident that an act of kindness or generosity would be reciprocated. Newcomers built permanent houses next to permanent neighbors, supported the same school and church, and saw their children marry the children of neighbors. Being on good terms with close neighbors was essential.

Settlers also built a network of social institutions to encourage cooperative behavior, the church being the most important example. However, fewer than 30 percent of rural dwellers were church members in the period from 1820–1860 (Johnson 1989, p. 182). In Allegany County, 75 churches reported that 9,833 souls, 25 percent of the local population, usually attended Sunday services (*Census, State of New York*, 1855, p.477). Certainly the evangelical church movement in the 1820s and 1830s testified that some community members were concerned about the wanton pursuit of worldly pleasures fu-eled by cheap whiskey (Johnson 1989, p. 115).

Much civility and kindness prevailed on the frontier, not because people were better then than now but because norms of reciprocity were well estab-lished among neighbors. Farm neighbors were an essential support system (Neth 1995, p. 41). Julia Tarbell Merrill writes that the social life of early set-tlers featured husking bees, spelling contests, barn raising, and hymn singing. Evening guest might expect a modest supper of potatoes and salt, sage tea and possibly a few small pieces of fried pork.

An early Fillmore area resident recalls, "When the date for a cabin rising was decided upon, word would go out to all the neighboring families that they must show up to help. When the day arrived the men would appear with good ox teams, logging chains and axes. It was the custom that the work began right after lunch, which the women brought with them and spread out on improvised tables of rough boards. . . . Each work gang was assigned to a specific job and they competed to see who could do the most work. A whiskey jug was passed around. At 6:00 p.m., women provided supper at the new settler's cabin and the workers returned home to complete their evening chores" (*Mouth of the Creek*, nd). The community encouraged neighbors to participate by limiting the work session to an afternoon and creating a festive atmosphere with food, drink and friendly competition.

The son of a physician recalled that doctors sometimes rode considerable distances to provide care for patients who could not afford to pay him, which reflects the customary spirit of community cooperation among early settlers. He reasoned, "If a man was sick, his neighbors planted, cultivated and harvested his crops freely, without pay. Why should not the physician doctor him without fees?" (Merrill 1908). The farm family often preferred to help neighbors directly than to trade with local shopkeepers. One farmer refused to sell his surplus potatoes to a passing stranger who offered a good price because "my neighbors are in need of them and can pay in work" (Merrill 1908, p. 76). Settlers were careful to keep the fire going in their cabin, but "going to the neighbors to borrow fire was no uncommon thing in those days" (Merrill 1908, p. 423).

Settlers used several strategies to encourage cooperative behavior within the community. Informal social sanctions were imposed on individuals who behaved badly. For example, settlers thought badly of anyone who did not show up on the appointed day to build a barn, repair a road or return a favor. A Rushford woman recalls that a failure to help your neighbor was long remembered in the community. "A woman, noting that her chimney made of mud covered sticks had caught on fire, hails a passing neighbor to extinguish the flames. He looked, offered the opinion that the fire would burn itself out, and went on. She climbed on the roof and put out the blaze herself. The man's laziness was for a long time a by word," concludes the storyteller (Merrill 1908).

These recollections may be romanticized, but early settlers had every incentive to build a community where trust, reciprocity and cooperation prevailed. On the frontier, opportunities to sell for cash were few. Participating fully in the life of the community and sharing labor and food with other families on a regular basis enabled people to live a richer life. Exchanging meat from hunting effort for some potatoes grown in a domestic garden built a deeper personal bond than did sale of goods or services for cash in the impersonal marketplace. In later decades, as market opportunities increased, a more individualistic spirit of getting ahead and pursuing ones self interest weakened these community ties (Sellers 1991).

POLITICS: LOCAL FACTIONS, WHIGS AND DEMOCRATS

Prior to 1828, Allegany County voters did not strongly identify with the principles of either Federalist or Jeffersonian Republican political parties or support party candidates consistently (Kass 1965; Gerber 1989). People voted for the individual candidate regardless of party before 1828, and local factional politics were more important than Federalist and Jeffersonian party principles (Shade 1981, p. 93). Victor Dupont captured the fluidity of local politics, "When I arrived here, I was given cause to doubt concerning the intention of Captain Church to take the turnpike in another direction away from my land. That made me quite upset with him. All the political parties had approached me trying to make me join. The ones who were opposed to Church offered to make me first judge. I wanted to remain neutral" (W3-691 January 7, 1807).

One local dispute pitted local residents against the Holland Land Company in 1806 and 1807 over whether a new Allegany County should be formed. Also at issue was whether legal proceedings should continue to be located in Geneva or whether they should be assigned to a new county court in Angelica in the newly formed county of Allegany. Dupont wrote to the New York State legislature,

"The Genesee County petitioners in requesting you to suspend the organization of Allegany County can have no other object but to oblige the citizens of the county to attend the court at Batavia and bear the expense and inconvenience to travel upwards of 80 miles in the most abominable roads. . . . These men are interested in the sale of the Holland Company's lands, not where it will best suit the inhabitants of Allegany County but where it will be most beneficial to the interest of said Holland Company. They show a spirit of domination and a wish to rule over their neighbors, which might be now the sentiment of most of the inhabitants of the Holland dominions in Europe but which ought never to prevail in America" (W3-693, January 22, 1807).

Another local issue, whether the county seat should be moved from Angelica to the Erie Railroad village of Belmont, divided the county in the 1850s. The economic center of the county was moving southward, but northern Allegany towns strongly opposed relocating the county seat further south. Belmont was a compromise location.

In national politics, Whigs and Democrats contested major elections after 1828, when Democrat Andrew Jackson was elected president, until 1856, when the conflict between north and south over the slavery issue dominated national politics. The old Jeffersonian Republicans formed the core of Democratic party support, while Federalist Party supporters gravitated to the Whigs. Elements of Whig and Democrat platforms appealed to different Allegany County voters. Local political entrepreneurs knitted together local factions as Whigs and Democrats. A growing population and improved transportation enabled local farmers to produce cash crops for the market and more shops opened their doors in the village. Issues of tariff protection and improving transportation had local meaning (Slade, 1981, p. 105). And by 1840, growing cultural diversity added another important dimension to politics. Protestant English and Scots immigrants identified with Whigs, while Irish and German Catholics tended to vote Democratic.

Three major issues divided Whigs and Democrats. First, proponents of individual freedom believed with Thomas Jefferson that government potentially meant tyranny. Democrats believed with Jefferson that the government that governs best is the one that governs least. Democrats thought that government had no business telling people what to believe, how to worship, and how to conduct their lives. Whigs believed that government should provide order in the community—a system of laws to protect property from the predations of envious neighbors, to discourage consumption of judgment impairing alcohol, and to promote schools that would teach right behavior (McCormick, 1966).

Second, nineteenth century Democrats believed that economic life should be governed by competition in the marketplace, free of governmental interference. Whigs believed that government should build public works projects that would stimulate economic growth. Whigs favored improvement of rivers and harbors, constructing canals and providing incentives to entrepreneurs willing to build new railroads.

Third, the two parties differed on the tariff question. Democrats favored free trade, while Whigs advocated protecting infant industries in America from competition from low cost manufacturers in England and elsewhere in Europe. Whigs believed that new American businesses needed protection from more efficient European producers, just as a healthy infant needs protection from the outside world until it matures and can stand on its own two feet.

How did Whigs and Democrats fare in Allegany County elections? The *Tribune Almanac* reports county level election statistics from 1838–1868. In most Allegany County elections from 1838 to 1854, Whigs or their allies consistently won contests for president, governor and U.S. Senate and House of Representative with 51 percent to 56 percent of the vote. The major exception was in 1852 when Democrat Zachary Taylor won a plurality of the Allegany County vote of president, as some normally Whig voters bolted to the Free Soil party over the slavery issue. Whigs did best in the villages and adjacent rural areas producing cash crops for market.

How might we explain the Whig dominance in Allegany County? First, Whigs were strong in New England, and many migrants to Allegany County in the 1830s and 1840s brought Whig sympathies with them. Second, improved transportation to New York City and the eastern seaboard was essential to economic prosperity in Allegany County. Locals agreed with the Whigs that government should support basic transportation infrastructure (Gunn 1988). Allegany County residents had paid taxes to build the Erie Canal in 1825. In 1850, they argued that state tax dollars should pay for the construction of the Genesee Valley Canal, for improvements in the Erie Canal, and to provide cheap land for the Erie Railroad right of way (Pierce 1953). In 1850, Allegany and other Southern Tier counties had considerable clout in state politics. These counties had reached their population peak, and their largest share of the New York State vote.

Third, the Whig position on tariffs appealed to the interests of Allegany County farmers, who in the 1840s practiced mixed farming with most of their produce consumed on the farm or sold in local markets. As Whig spokesman Horace Greeley made the case for protectionism,

> "The change from Free Trade to Protection inevitably brings markets for his own products nearer to his farm, increasing their cash value and extending his range of profitable production. . . . He begins to feel the stimulus of near markets urging him to produce other articles far more profitable than wheat growing for the English market. Should a manufactory of any kind be established within a few miles of him, he finds there a market for wood, vegetables, poultry, fresh butter and hay. . . . He improves his buildings and thus gives a job to his neighbor the carpenter, he fills up his house with furniture to the satisfaction of his neighbor the cabinet maker" (*Whig Almanac 1852*, p. 11).

The Democratic gospel of free trade appealed to export-oriented southern cotton farmers and Midwestern wheat producers, who feared that European states would impose retaliatory tariffs on these agricultural exports. Also, southern and Midwestern communities could purchase manufactured goods at lower prices if English factories were allowed to compete with American producers.

Fourth, Whigs were promoters of order and right behavior, supporting Protestant church going and temperance, which struck a responsive chord in Allegany County. Hard drinking, Catholic Irish laborers who worked to build roads, railroad and canal in Allegany County in the 1840s and 1850s had many local enemies. The Irish population identified with the Democratic Party statewide, which did not increase its appeal in Allegany County.

Whigs faded quickly from the political scene in the early 1850s. In Allegany County some Whig supporters voted for the anti-Catholic Know Nothing Party in 1854, demonstrating the strength of anti-Irish sentiment. But that issue was quickly eclipsed by the coming conflict between North and South over the slavery question. Democrats were divided on the anti slavery issue nationally, while Whigs were outflanked by the new Republican Party on the slavery issue.

TAMING NATURE AND BUILDING HOMES

Native Americans generally worked within the constraints imposed by nature. Early settlers ruthlessly transformed nature to meet their needs. They cut down trees, converting forest to crop land and pasture and wiped out the threatening wolves. How did they justify this confident, frontal attack on nature? The answer lies in the settler's belief that God had created man in his image and given man the intellect to exercise domination over the earth and its creatures (Cronon 1983). In both Federal and Greek Revival architectural styles, for example, settlers celebrated their ability to conquer and dominate the natural world, converting forest into pasture and replacing wolves with milk cows. Man was the dominant species, created in the image of God and given dominion over all of earth's creatures. Settlers incorporated into their homes classical Roman and Greek ideas of balance, proportion and symmetry, demonstrating the power of their intellect.

Roman and Greek accomplishments indicated what humans could achieve, and Roman and Greek architectural ideas appeared in early western New York farm houses. The first clapboard houses constructed in Allegany County from about 1810–1825 were mostly built in the Federalist style, which was

This well preserved Federalist style house is located in Alfred Station in the Susquehanna River valley, settled at an early date (author's photo).

inspired by the architectural ideas of ancient Rome and the Italian Renaissance. Families valued more space, and the Federal style home allowed for two full floors (Small 1997). Houses built in the early nineteenth century all over western New York look a lot like this representative Federalist house that features a strong sense of balance and proportion. Two window bays flank the central doorway, which is usually surrounded by small sidelights. Inside are a central hall and four rooms.

The small pane windows are shuttered against the weather. The ridge of the gable roof runs parallel to the front of the building and the road. The writers of builder's manuals and newspaper articles who popularized the Federalist style were very much influenced by the architectural and political ideas of Robert Adam in England and Thomas Jefferson in the United States (Clark 1986). Early travelers in central New York named towns like Ithaca, Syracuse, Marcellus, Cicero and Romulus after Roman places and people. In Allegany County, Cuba may be named for a lesser Roman deity who was the protector of infants asleep in their cradles. The Allegany County town of Ceres recalls the Roman goddess of grain.

Politically, Roman constitutional principles were crucially important. Romans established the rule of law and the concept that power should be divided. As the Roman Senate checked the power of the Caesar, so the English Parliament was to check the power of the English monarch. That was the meaning of the Glorious Revolution of 1688, when Parliament invited William and Mary to occupy the English throne, with the understanding that the monarch served at the pleasure of Parliament elected by the English people (Clifford 1986).

Educated Americans in 1776, most of who had emigrated from England, asserted the principle that a tyrannous English government had no right to tax the American colonists without granting them representation in Parliament. The rallying cry of the American war for independence, no taxation without representation, was familiar to the oldest residents of Allegany County in 1820 and their children. In 1789, the Founding Fathers incorporated Roman ideas of balance and proportion in crafting the new American Constitution, which divided power among three branches of government and set up an elaborate system of checks and balances.

The grand Georgian homes built by the English landed gentry, by the coastal commercial elite in Annapolis and Philadelphia and by Southern plantation owners in the eighteenth century, before the revolutionary war for independence, is the high style expression of these architectural ideas. The chimneys at the end of the building signal that the owners could afford to have a fireplace to heat every room.

Philip Church built this elegant but restrained home at Belvidere on the shores of the Genesee River. Its Georgian style was fashionable among English landowners of the day. The well proportioned entrance with sidelights is topped by an oval eyebrow window. Multiple chimneys at the corners are a feature of Georgian homes (author's photo).

Wealthy Allegany County landowner Philip Church built the original Turnpike Road from Almond to Angelica in 1810, subsidized saw mills, merchants and blacksmiths to attract the first wave of settlers to the county, and sold parcels of land to these early settlers. The balance and proportion revealed in these early nineteenth century Federalist homes reflect settler confidence that they were doing God's will in imposing their will on the disorderly natural world.

Today, a few original Federal style homes remain in those Allegany towns like Almond, Alfred and especially Angelica that were settled earliest. On the frontier, many settlers did not have particularly good carpenter skills, and their Federal style homes have not survived. Other Federal style homes have burned. The town of Rushford centennial reports that 63 homes in Rushford village were devoured by flames in the first 100 years. If we count about 100 homes in nineteenth century Rushford, any early house has over a 60 percent chance of going up in flames by 1900. A few Federal style houses still sit in the oldest sections of the oldest towns, but owners have modernized them many times over 180 years, changing the roof line, adding rooms and changing windows so that we can no longer easily see the original federalist structure.

By 1840, 40,000 settlers had poured into Allegany County. This period of heavy settlement coincided with a shift in interest among educated Americans from republican Rome to democratic Greece. Andrew Jackson, elected president in 1828, was a popular figure among frontier farmers who were suspicious of commercial elites, town bankers and large landowners who had dominated politics during the first decades of the new republic. The people increasingly admired Athenian democracy, where all citizens met in the public market place and shared in making decisions about public life. Every man ought to cast a ballot and participate in public affairs. Americans who had just completed their own war for independence against a colonial oppressor, cheered the struggle of contemporary Greeks for independence from the Turks (Gelertner 1999).

In western New York, settlers now incorporated ideas taken from Greek temple architecture into the American farm house. The roof gable was turned 90 degrees so that the smaller side of the house fronted on the street, giving the farm house a temple-like appearance.

The columns supported a triangular pediment beneath a wide cornice. More commonly, a flat façade featured corner pilasters that resembled columns and appeared to support a triangular pediment. A wide cornice, often with grills over small windows, supported the roof. Most commonly, Greek revival farm houses were painted white to resemble the stone Greek temple originals.

Of course, hardworking Allegany County farmers were not really close students of the contributions of the Greeks to democracy or of the meaning of

This grand version of Greek revival architecture, constructed in 1867 after the Civil War, features fluted columns with Ionic capitals supporting a triangular pediment, creating a sheltered portico in the manner of the Southern plantation (author's photo).

classical Greek architecture. But builder's manuals and agricultural magazines were widely disseminated by 1830. Articles informed homebuilders
why classical Greek ideas of democracy were so relevant for contemporary
Americans, spread the news about this latest current architectural fashion, and
offered construction tips. Greek revival architectural motifs dominate in western New York from about 1825 to about 1850.

In a typical western New York village, the oldest Greek revival houses are
found along a street running along a valley floor bordering a stream. The
name of the street reflects its importance—State, Main, or perhaps the name
of the neighboring village to which it connects. In villages located at the in-
tersection of two valleys, a second "main street" intersects the first. Core
neighborhoods along Main Street are the oldest neighborhoods.

The focus on Greek democracy did not serve Allegany County farm
women particularly well. While males discussed the political issues of the day
and voted in elections, women were excluded from participating in community public affairs. Some males who did the excluding justified their actions
by reference to Greek practice. Elizabeth Cady Stanton, Susan B. Anthony,
Lucretia Mott and other women met at Seneca Falls in 1848 to protest the
subordination of women. But for decades to come, the influence of women
was largely confined to home and family. Not until 1917 did women win the
right to vote in New York State (Baker 1991, p. 148).

The dominant Greek revival style faded in popularity after 1850. Builder's
manuals asserted that temple architecture was an unsuitable model for private
homes. To the critics, bare, bald Greek revival cubes clashed with the darker
hues and complexity of the natural landscape. To practical western New York
farmers, grandeur is appropriate for building a church to worship the Lord,
but not for a farm house where people eat, sleep and work.

Another domestic architecture style, Gothic Revival, underlines the importance of religion in the everyday life of the western New York farm family. Gothic revival building drew its inspiration from the Gothic cathedrals of
Europe. The soaring towers, pointed window arches and steeply gabled roof
of Gothic construction draws the eye upward. It celebrates not human intellect and accomplishment but the quest for divine inspiration and support. Ver-
tical board and batten siding accentuates the pointed window arches and
steeply gabled roof and draws the eye upward, toward the heavens.

Gothic cottages were popular because at mid-century, the Christian church
was a main center of community life. Most people were newcomers, and the
church was central to building a sense of community. The fabric of laws governing individual behavior was thin and few local law officers were paid to
enforce them. The church encouraged community members to live moral up-
right lives and warned wrongdoers of divine retribution. The church discour-

This Gothic cottage in Cuba features decorative tracery in the center gable (author's photo)

aged wrong behavior—fighting to resolve disputes, cheating others in business deals, drinking alcohol. The Gothic cottage presents the home as a Christian sanctuary and affirms the importance of Christian values.

After 1850, transportation improvements transformed economic and social life in western New York. The next chapter examines changes in farm and village life at mid-century.

NOTES

1. It is worth noting the cautionary significance of this story in 1881, when foreclosure threatened farmers in the grip of economic recession.

2. The D'Autremont letters in English translation, written from 1805 to 1807, are available at the Angelica Public Library. Marie writes, "Boards cost here four dollars for a thousand feet. Mr. Church, who has the sawing mill, refuses to sell any. There are sawing mills at twenty or twenty five miles from here, but what bad roads." (March 13 1806) Phillip Church apparently kept his business and social life separate.

Chapter Four

The Western New York Farm at Mid-Century

The transition from clearing the land to cash crop farming in western New York was well underway by the 1850s. Rapid population growth, improvements in transportation, and greater agricultural productivity stimulated the transition to cash crop farming. The New York State Census of 1855 provides detailed information about who lived on a typical Allegany County farm, what the farmhouse looked like, and how farmers used their land.

TRANSITION FROM SUBSISTENCE TO CASH CROP FARMING

The rural population in Allegany County grew steadily from about 19,400 in 1830 to 41,600 in 1855 when New York State conducted the first thorough and somewhat reliable census. County population actually declined from 41,597 in 1855 to 40,285 in 1865, with population declining in 24 of the county's 29 towns. Belfast and Caneadea lost over 20 percent of their populations when workers moved away after completion of the Genesee Valley Canal. As farm land increased in price, sons of farmers moved west in search of land to clear or to the growing Erie Canal cities.

Some small farmers sold out to new dairy farmers who needed more pasture land, some laborers moved on after completing canal and railroad construction, and about 585 men who went off to fight in the Civil War never returned. The only towns to gain population were the rugged southern hill towns of Alma, Andover, Clarksville and Genesee, then being logged following completion of railroad and canal, and Wellsville, rapidly emerging as the county commercial center.

After 1850, the productivity of western New York farmers increased dramatically. Newly established farmers were still engaged in clearing the land and planting crops primarily for household use. Older, better established farms were specializing in more profitable dairy production. The 1855 New York State Census places the average value of all Allegany County farms at $2,241; the average value of farms involved in cheese production was $3,463—one third higher. Heads of household producing cheese were older (47) than the average head of household (41) and had been working the land for much longer (22 years) than the average head of household (14 years) (New York State Census 1855). The transition to dairying did not take place at the same rate in all Allegany County towns. Towns located in the flat river valleys where soils were fertile were centers of economic activity. Hillside towns were economic backwaters where seasonal loggers were still clearing the land in the 1850s.

Early farmers in western New York had practiced safety first agriculture, their goal being to feed and clothe their family whatever unpredictable weather and markets might bring. Self sufficiency, subsistence crop production and mixed farming received high priority. Markets were not well developed, and prices fluctuated wildly. Before railroad and canal, prohibitive transportation costs lowered the price the farmer could expect for his surplus grain or livestock and raised the price of imported coffee and hardware.

In this situation, farmers calculated that they were better off sharing their surplus with neighbors and bartering with local store keepers, who would in turn be called upon to help the farmer's family in time of need. This ethic of community cooperation was well established until mid-century, when many Allegany farmers had completed the process of clearing the land. They were learning about ways to increase yields per acre, and specializing in producing surplus crops, especially dairy, for sale in the marketplace. By 1865, the western New York frontier had given way to settled agriculture in many towns. Railroad and canal dramatically reduced transportation costs and connected Allegany County farmers to distant markets. Many farmers had shifted from general mixed farming to specialized dairy production and were bringing larger quantities of raw milk to local cheese factories. By 1869 New York had established its position as the number one dairy state, accounting for 57 percent of all US milk production.

Several developments made this transition possible. First, improved transportation expanded market opportunities for farm households. At the local level, the roads connecting farms and nearby villages improved in quality. In 1841, some 302 peddlers were licensed in the state of New York; in 1855 that number increased to 4,131 (Jaffee 1991). Part of that increase is due to more accurate counting, but increase is also due to decreasing transportation costs as roads were improved. Farm families now bartered their surplus in exchange for the peddler's goods.

The roads connecting major villages along turnpikes and canals improved steadily. At their peak around 1840, about 270 turnpikes operated in New York State, crowded with passenger-carrying stage coaches, ox-drawn freight wagons, itinerant peddlers, flocks of turkeys and herds of livestock. These turnpikes were exciting places, promoting easy sociability among passersby punctuated with occasional incidents of road rage. By 1850, privately owned toll-charging turnpikes in western New York had largely faded into history. Users had every incentive to evade the toll gate and, therefore, the cost of collecting tolls was high (Taylor 1962, p. 28). Free public roads were steadily improving in quality. And canals and railroads were rapidly emerging as a long distance travel alternative to the turnpike.

Construction of the Erie Canal, completed in 1825, opened up the upper Genesee Valley. No private investors could know whether a canal into the wilderness would lower transportation costs enough to stimulate commercial prosperity and provide a return on their investment. Few private corporations were amassing capital in 1817, when construction began. New York State provided all of the construction funds; other states that stood to benefit from low cost access to east coast markets from Buffalo passed resolutions of encouragement but offered no financial backing (Goodrich 1960 p. 53).

The Erie Canal was profitable from the outset and paid off its debt by 1836. The canal was relatively cheap to construct and operate because the elevation gain from the Hudson River to Buffalo through the Mohawk Valley was small and the supply of water ample. By contrast, feeder canals like the Genesee Valley Canal had to cross hilly terrain and relied on man-made reservoirs like Cuba Lake at higher elevations (Taylor 1951, p. 34; p. 155). Ultimately, the canals could not compete with railroads. Their narrow shallow waters carried a small volume of traffic, operation and maintenance costs were high, and canals could not operate at all during the frozen winter months and during late summer droughts (Taylor 1951 p. 52-55).

Completion of the Genesee Valley Canal and the Erie Railroad by 1856 dramatically reduced transportation costs and fully integrated Allegany County into the regional market economy. In the more remote Allegany County towns, lumbering increased as the cost of transporting logs and lumber to ready markets along the Erie Canal and the Atlantic Seaboard fell dramatically. The towns of Alma and New Hudson, originally populated by a few hundred isolated souls scratching out a subsistence living were joined by a new generation of lumberjacks. In 1853, 14 million feet of lumber lined the banks of the new canal in Belfast, awaiting shipment northward to Rochester (McNall 1952, p. 189).

The major east-west railroad, the Erie, connected the Allegany County farmer with New York City and Buffalo. Wellsville and Angelica fought hard to persuade Jay Gould to lay the Erie Railroads tracks through their communities. The possible route through Angelica was only 25 miles from Hornell to Belmont, but the steep grade required making a deep cut through the West Almond hill. Gould lacked the capital to pursue the idea, and Angelica residents ultimately rejected Gould's suggestion that they pay most of the cost of constructing the new rail bed (*Allegany County Republican* January 1, 1882). Gould chose to route the Erie from Hornell to Belmont through Wellsville, spreading the elevation gain over an additional 13 miles. The decision ensured that Wellsville, not Angelica, would become the economic center of Allegany County.

The railroad was the centerpiece of the local economy, tying rural villages to Rochester and Buffalo. Railroads were widely seen as a key to economic prosperity; even vested interests like wagon makers and teamsters recognized that the railroad increased short haul travel from farm to railroad station (Taylor 1951 p. 156). The Pittsburgh, Shawmut and Northern (PSN) carried coal from Pennsylvania to rural villages in western New York, but the financially strapped railroad never completed track to the Erie Canal cities.

The PSN located its workshops in Angelica, where it employed up to 145 men plus 40 administrative staff and train operators. The automobile had a devastating impact on the railroad; local detractors who used its passenger service called the PSN the "pretty slow and noisy." Rail employment declined after World War I, passenger service was discontinued in 1936, the PSN shops closed in 1939, and the railroad would operate its last train in 1945.

Progressives in local communities were eager to invest in rail service to their town, hoping the railroad would convert their village into a city and double or triple land values. When the 1846 state constitution prohibited the state from lending money to private corporations, capital-hungry railroads sought credit from city, village and town governments. The Panic of 1873 plunged many short haul railroads into bankruptcy, and local government bonds were worthless. The towns of Amity, Angelica, Birdsall, Caneadea and Hume lost an average of $440,000 on the short lived Buffalo and Belmont and the Rochester, Nunda and Pennsylvania railroads (Pierce 1953). Advocates of keeping taxes low and mistrusting government cited this bitter experience.

Agricultural innovation also spurred the transition from subsistence oriented farming to specialized cash crop farming, primarily dairy. Harrow, seed drill, cultivator and threshing machine were among inventions that transformed agriculture. In 1850, about 1,000 patents were granted nationwide; in 1860 five times as many patents were granted. The shift from oxen to horses as draft animals also increased agricultural productivity. While oxen

This model of a hay wagon was patented by an Allegany County farmer in 1869. Many farmers at mid-century were eager to adopt new and improved agricultural practice (Hinkle Library, Alfred State College.)

are better for lumbering activities, horses worked more quickly in plowing and planting cleared fields. Two men with a pair of oxen could plow half an acre per day; one man with a pair of horses could plow four acres. Information about new technologies and better farming practices was widely disseminated in practical magazines for farmers and in demonstrations at local fairs (Hedrick 1933).

What were the consequences of the spread of cash crop farming? First, villages became more active places, as shops offered a broader range of goods and services and small workshops transformed lumber into cabinets, hides into leather goods and milk into cheese. Second, individual farmers were selling lumber and dairy products and pocketing the cash for their own use (Brooks 1996; Sellers 1991). Traditional close ties among neighbors based upon sharing what a farm household produced, holding barn raisings and quilting bees to lighten work, providing moral support to neighbors in time of need were weakened. Farmers were tempted to maximize their own incomes by producing for the cash market rather than to promote community solidarity through shared work.

As market relations deepened, traditional ties between neighbors were put to the test. A local farmer and the village blacksmith, for example, often developed a friendly business relationship. The blacksmith might shoe an impoverished farmer's horse in exchange for the farmer's gratitude, a promise to bring some meat when the pig was slaughtered, and an invitation to the fall harvest festival. When farmer and blacksmith had a long future together, each player could keep count, each had an incentive to maintain good relations with their neighbor, and each received a (3) in their social game. By mid-century, these traditional ties were strained. Should the farmer continue to visit the blacksmith when high quality, low-cost hardware manufactured in factories was now available at the general store? (Summerhill 2005, p. 102). In this Prisoner's Dilemma game, the farmer was tempted to abandon the local blacksmith. Both players had received a score of (3), but now the farmer could do better (4) at the expense of the blacksmith (1).

In the household division of labor in western New York, the man worked the fields. His more highly valued labor was devoted to field crops, which absorbed most of the productivity-improving capital investment. The woman managed the household and produced a substantial portion of the household income through feeding livestock, gathering wood, and preserving food. In the early years of dairying, the exhausting, time-consuming labor of milking cows and making cheese was added to women's traditional home chores. Hand milking required about seven minutes per cow twice daily, which added up to 2.3 hours per day for 10 cows and 3.5 hours per day for a 15 cow herd.

This factory converted raw milk into condensed milk and cream. Cans of condensed milk and cream now await shipment on the next train to wholesalers in New York and other cities (Allegany County Historian).

Feeding, herding and sanitation required additional daily labor. The cheese making process required considerable strength and skill. Because women, older family members and young children did most of the dairying work, the opportunity cost of labor was low. Women cheese makers were commonly hired at $2 per week plus board. Farm and dairy literature that celebrated the enormous profitability of dairying focused on the value of the dairy output, not on the value of labor diverted from other household tasks (Bateman 1968).

The spread of dairy farming also changed the relationship between husband and wife within the household. Why did women add dairying operations and cheese making to their list of contributions to the household economy? An exploitation theory argues that men's physical strength, patriarchal cultural values and superior legal/political position forced their women to contribute a larger share to the household economy. Social reformers by 1860 were protesting the added work that dairying imposed on the farm woman. They championed a traditional household division of labor in which the male would earn the family bread and women would raise the children and manage the home—a concept widely accepted among prosperous middle class families by the 1880s. A problem with this exploitation theory is that cheese making improved the farm woman's quality of life and strengthened her bargaining position within the household. Long days were a constant for the nineteenth century farm woman, and she was better off laboring in the cheese making room than at the spinning wheel and the loom as her mother had—so long as she had some control of the income from her cheese making (Jensen 1986).

A second theory argues that males had to provide their wives with incentives to take on yet one more arduous chore. The farm woman in 1840 typically created the product, controlled the marketing and handled the money while her husband worked in forest and fields (McMurry 1995). With the cash from the sale of cheese, she could purchase more and better goods at lower prices and be spared the tedium of making soap, cloth and candles at home. Viewed in this way, women did well to accept the burden of cheese making on the family farm. They worked as hard as ever, but their labor diversified their family's diet and raised income from the sale of surplus butter and cheese (Osterud 1991, p. 13).[1]

THE VILLAGE AS COMMERCIAL CENTER

Census gatherers did not count the population of villages until 1890. However, information about early village populations may be gleaned from Beer's

1869 *Atlas of Allegany County.* Beer provides scale maps of 39 villages recording the location of every business and residence. The village populations for 1869 are estimated by counting the residences in each village and multiplying by five, the average number of household members recorded in the 1855 New York State census. Table 4.1 shows the estimated distribution of villages by population size in 1869.

Together, about 27 percent of Allegany County residents lived in these 39 widely scattered villages in 1865. Seven villages had over 500 residents, all located along railroad or canal. Wellsville village contained about 1,250 residents, or three percent of the county population. Two-thirds of the villages had fewer than 250 residents, and people were already making the wagon trip or taking the train to larger villages offering a wider range of goods and services.

Most of the new ideas about housing styles and organization of household space originated in the villages. Before the Civil War, farm families built their homes in Federal and Greek revival styles, and their children enlarged and adapted the original structures. New ideas about domestic architecture appeared in the villages after the Civil War. English travelers described in popular journals their impressions of the Italian countryside. They were captivated by the charm of sun drenched hillsides, peasants following their seasonal routines, the quiet serenity of a landscape unspoiled by the harshness of the industrial revolution. Italianate and Italian Villa housing styles soon filled the builder's manuals and popular journals in England and America. A romantic spirit that recalled traditional values of an idyllic past, and valued the dark hues and irregularities of the natural landscape, replaced the rational spirit of the Enlightenment with its emphasis on balance and proportion in architecture. Most farmhouses were already completed by the time Italianate became fashionable, although after the Civil War many Greek revival houses were updated with Italianate features.

Italianate houses are more common and easily recognized. A hipped roof with four planes meeting at the crown of the roof replaces the gable roof of Federal and Greek revival styles. Ornately carved brackets support wide roof

Table 4.1.   Estimated Population Size, Allegany County Villages, 1869

Village Population	N	%
Under 99	10	26%
100–249	15	38%
250–449	7	18%
Over 50	7	18%
Total	39	100%

A mid century Italianate house in the village of Cuba (author's photo).

overhangs. Heavy decorative stone lintels surround the windows. The first floor is taller than the second; interior ceilings can be 13 feet high and very long windows adorn the first floor. Carved woodwork dresses the porch that surrounds the entrance.

Interior organization of space was of greater practical importance than external architectural detail. In the early farm house, the large multi-purpose kitchen was a unified workplace located at the rear of the house overlooking fields and farm yard. From this command post, women prepared food, watched small children, made cheese and entertained visitors (McMurry 1988, p. 209).

By mid century, Allegany County industry largely consisted of processing the principal resources of the area—grain, timber and animal hides—and most of these workshops were located in villages. Table 4.2 shows that the number of establishments increased by 10 percent from 1840 to 1855, and these establishments were becoming more specialized.

The 1840 economy largely consisted of sawing lumber, grinding grain and processing hides. By 1855, local incomes earned cutting timber and producing butter and cheese also supported new consumer industries. People improved their roofs, dressed up their windows and installed cabinets to contain their swelling possessions. The number of gristmills declined from 1840 to 1855 as flour was increasingly milled at the High Falls area of Rochester and

A tower, an irregular roof line, and an off-centered entrance are characteristic of Italian Villa construction, as in this example located in the village of Bolivar. In later decades, owners often removed towers as they fell into disrepair (author's photo).

Table 4.2. Principal Manufactures in Allegany County, 1840 and 1855

Manufacturing Category	Number	1840	%	Number	1855	%
Furnace and forge	6		2.0%	4		1.2%
Tin and sheet iron	—			8		2.4%
Sash and blind	—			4		1.2%
Coach and wagon	—			29		8.6%
Grist mill	39		12.6%	23		6.8%
Lumber products	—			15		4.5%
Saw mills	204		66.0%	183		54.5%
Boots and shoes	—			23		6.8%
Harness makers	—			13		3.9%
Tanneries	30		9.7%	17		5.1%
Cabinet making	—			13		3.9%
Gunsmith	—			4		1.2%
Distilleries	2		.6%	—		
Cloth manufacture	28		9.1%	—		
Total	309		100.0%	336		100.1%

Source: Census of 1840 reported in John Disturnell, Disturnell's Gazetteer, Albany, 1842; New York State Census of 1855.

shipped eastward on the Erie Canal. Inexpensive cotton cloth was by 1855 manufactured at large factories in New England.[2]

The 1840 Census reports 204 sawmills on the rivers and creeks of Allegany County. Most of these sawmills cut small amounts of timber for local consumption, the average annual product of these small mills being less than $1,000. Abolitionist Frederick Douglas, who gave a series of anti-slavery lectures in Allegany County in October 1851, observed, "Sawmills are dotted all over Allegany's valleys and so profitable is the lumber business that many of the men engaged in it think it more for their interest to buy the produce than to cultivate their lands, of which they have abundance. Timber is to Allegany what gold is to California, and these must be exhausted before there will be much cultivation of the soil in either" (accessible.palinet.org/scripts)

Most businesses in 1855 were sawmills, at a time when the settlers were replacing their original log cabins with clapboard sided houses. Only Granger, Grove and West Almond had no sawmills in 1855. Until the 1850s, water power was cheaper than steam power in western New York; logs or grain needed to be transported only a few miles to a nearby saw or grist mill

Wiscoy creek was the site of an early productive saw mill. A sluice carried water from about 100 yards upstream to the water wheel next to the building at the right that contained the machinery. Only the building now remains (author's photo).

Table 4.3. **Allegany County Occupations, 1865**

Occupation	Number	Percentage
Farmers	7342	67.1%
Machinists, carpenters, blacksmiths, shoemakers, barrel makers, other crafts	1624	14.8%
Laborers	579	5.3%
Merchants, teachers, lawyers, physicians, clergy	589	5.4%
Servants	412	3.8%
Other	397	3.6%
Total	10,943	100%

Source: 1865 Census

located on a local stream (Temin 1966). These sawmills were much larger and more efficient than the typical sawmill a decade earlier.

Efficient sawmill operation required well forested hills that absorbed water during spring snow melt and heavy rainfall periods and released the water gradually into rivers and streams. The annual variation in water flow is lessened, as creeks did not become raging torrents in April nor did they dry up in August. By the middle of the nineteenth century, many Allegany towns were deforested and the land converted to field crop and pasture. Forest trees had once held the soil during heavy rains, slowing the rate of runoff into creeks and rivers and minimizing soil erosion (Whitney 1994).

After deforestation, water raced down the hills during heavy rains, carrying away the soil with it. When major floods struck Allegany County towns, homes and businesses, often located in the floodplain along the banks of creeks, suffered heavy damage. Raging waters frequently destroyed saw mill sites. The water behind the dam constantly nibbled away at the shore in search of a way around the dam. Flash floods accelerated this erosion process to dams along mill streams. A major flood in 1855 wiped out numerous small sawmills in Allegany County. None survived the flood of 1897. Notable floods in 1861, 1865, and 1889 and 1972 also caused much erosion in fields and damage to structures in low lying areas. Floods and drought provided a powerful impetus for lumbermen to harness their saws to steam engines.

One-third of the Allegany County work force provided non-farm goods and services at the time of the Civil War. The 1865 Census identifies 27 occupational categories, indicating greater specialization and more economic activity. The new railroads employed 114 workers and Allegany County residents had enough money to support 67 wagon makers and 38 milliners.

A SNAPSHOT OF TYPICAL FARMS IN 1855

Dairy farming was established earlier in some Allegany County towns than in others. Prior to completion of the Erie Canal in 1825, the economic center of Allegany County lay in the Susquehanna River basin towns of Almond and Alfred. By 1855, economic advantage had shifted to towns along the Genesee Valley Canal and the Erie Railroad. These towns tended to have more diverse economies with numerous industrial workshops and village businesses, reflecting the importance of cheap transportation for successful economic growth. In these towns, the transition to dairy was well underway, and cows now grazed in the pastures that replaced the original forest. In towns further removed from rail and canal, lumbering continued to dominate the local economy. Small numbers of lumbermen and subsistence farmers supported only a few workshops and businesses.

The large quantity of detailed information in the 1855 Census presents a snapshot of the Allegany County farm at mid century. The fragile, handwritten original census pages are hard to read; the paper and binding deteriorate with each passing year. Fortunately, one local historian about 20 years ago painstakingly made a typescript of the 1855 Census for the towns of Centerville, Granger, and Hume. This typescript is located in the Jean Lang Historical Collection at Alfred State College, Alfred, NY. However, the valuable information about who lived in an Allegany County farmhouse, where the occupants were born, and how long they lived in Allegany County was not analyzed.

In 2002, an Alfred University student, Mark McGovern made an even more important advance. Choosing six diverse towns representing all three Allegany County watersheds, McGovern patiently transcribed data from the 1855 census into an electronic database containing over 12,000 records for 1900 households, which is now available to historical researchers (McGovern and Rasmussen 2003). What can 1855 Census data tell us about the background and lives of people in Allegany County households? The Census reports information about material used to build houses, value of housing, who lived in farm households, their age, gender and relationship to the head of household, and birthplace of the head of household.

Table 4.4 shows that by 1855, one generation after initial settlement, about 15 percent of farmers in Centerville, Granger and Hume continued to live in their original log cabins, while the rate for all of Allegany County was only eight percent. These log cabins were distributed widely among the 29 towns and had an average value of $39, while wood framed houses had an average value of $403. Clearly, Allegany County people did not want to live in log cabins, even though they were available at bargain basement prices. Contributors to the centennial memorial history, *Allegany and Its People* could identify only six log cabins still inhabited in 1896. The census of 1855 reports an average of 5.5 inhabitants per dwelling-too many to be cramped in a small log cabin.

Within a decade of settlement, a saw mill on every decent sized stream in Allegany County reduced bulky logs to support timbers and clapboard siding. A framed house yielded more usable space; often four rooms on the first floor, including kitchen, dining room and parlor in which to receive visitors and possibly a bedroom for the head of the household and his wife. A second floor provided additional bedrooms and storage space.

Table 4.4. Material of House, Three Late Settled Towns, 1855

Material of House	Allen		Centerville		Granger	
	N	%	N	%	N	%
Log	24	12%	35	14%	51	20%
Frame	166	85%	222	85%	197	79%
Other	6	3%	3	1%	3	1%
Total	196	100%	260	100%	251	100%

Source: New York State Census, Allegany County, 1855.

This New England salt box style log cabin, photographed about 1910, dates from about 1804. This style house with its long sloped roof was already out of fashion by 1800 and very few were built in Allegany County. Full logs make up the ground floor. A door was the only original opening. In a very few years, a second story was fashioned out of clapboard siding with window (Allegany County Historian).

Balloon frame construction developed in the 1830s using 2 x 4 boards at eighteen inch intervals, made possible lighter, stronger and more flexible construction (Clark 1986). Balloon frame construction required efficient saw mills to produce standard lumber, kegs of low cost nails, and cheap transportation. Balloon framing quickly replaced the practice of constructing a wall on the ground, using heavy planks, hand cut pegs and mortise and tenon joints, and then lifting the wall into place (Wright 1981; Peterson 1992).

The whole construction process did not require much cash. Owners typically had little access to capital, bank mortgage financing not being available until the 1900s. Labor dominated the cost of construction. The owner typically cut the trees, dragged them to a nearby sawmill, carted the lumber back to the construction site, and enlisted the help of neighbors to erect the house. Still, building houses was a major investment in pre Civil War Allegany County and western New York. The market value of labor was about one dollar per day, or $300 per year, and the 1855 Census records the average value of an Allegany County home at about $300. Thus the value of a house was almost a year's income, although the farm family did not need much cash to support construction activity.

Who lived in the houses that dotted the hills of Allegany County in 1855? The census taker recorded relevant information, which is summarized in Table 4.5 for the towns of Allen, Centerville and Granger. On average, over five persons lived in a typical house.

About 70 percent of households consisted of nuclear family members only—husband, wife and children. Clearly, the demographic transition to having few children was well underway on the western New York farm by 1855; a family was more likely to have two or three children than five or six.

Table 4.5.   Household Composition, Allegany County Farms, 1855

Household Members	Allen		Centerville		Granger	
	N	%	N	%	N	%
Nuclear family members	978	94%	1330	92%	1117	94%
Aging parents	8	—	35	2%	19	2%
Laborer, servant, boarder	21	2%	18	1%	24	2%
Brother, sister, grandchild	29	3%	60	4%	24	2%
Total	1036		1443		1180	
Mean household members	5.3		5.5		4.7	
% households with non nuclear family residents	30%		43%		25%	

Source: Compiled by author from the typescript of the 1855 Census for the towns of Allen, Centerville and Granger, Jean Lang Historical Collection, Alfred State College.

Why were farm families having fewer children? Historically in agricultural societies, infant mortality rates of farm families were high and life expectancy was low for those who did reach their fifth birthday. Inadequate nutrition and exposure to water born disease exacted their toll on human life spans. In this setting where death rates were high, families had as many children as possible. Children were a low cost labor supply who contributed more to the farm economy than the cost of their upkeep. By the mid-nineteenth century, a demographic transition had taken place on the western New York farm. Farm adults were living longer and choosing to give birth to fewer children. Farm families calculated that the marginal cost of children exceeded the value of their contribution to the farm (Easterlin 1976; Leet 1976).

In 1855, about 4,400 farms were developed in Allegany County and the population included 4,500 young males between the ages of 10 and 20 who would be looking for a farm to own. But few farms were available. Many aging parents in good health would not be ready to turn over their farms to a son. Most of the best land was already cleared and available for sale at unaffordable prices. Some of Allegany County's sons climbed on the train to seek employment in the growing cities or moved west in search of cheap land to clear as their fathers had done before them.

Allegany County's population held constant for over a century because more young men were migrating out of Allegany County than in, and because farm families were choosing to have smaller families. Fathers felt obligated to share the value of the farm among their sons, but the farm could only support one son's family. Finding the cash to set up a second or third son with a farm near the family homestead was an expensive proposition in 1855. In a low inflation environment, the price of land more than doubled from 1836 to 1855.

Farm families in western New York came to think that the ideal family would be one son, who would inherit the family farm, and one daughter, who would marry an established widowed farmer or the son of a farming neighbor, or a tradesman in the nearby village. A farmer could hire additional labor as needed rather than raise his own labor supply. Rather than feeding additional children, family income was better spent purchasing improved plows, small engines and other agricultural technology.

Farm ownership typically passed from father to son. Daughters were never given control of their father's farm in 1855; they often married a neighboring farmer and moved to his farm. Older men had more years to build up their farm; therefore they were desirable marriage partners for younger women. Most commonly, control of the farm had passed from an aging parent or parents to their son, and the aging parents continued to live on the farm. In one case from the town of Granger, 15 year old Samuel Bennett was counted as

This photo, taken a generation after 1855, is demographically appropriate. The farmer, his spouse and their three children live in the main house to the right. The grandparents who probably grew up in this Greek revival house built about 1835 still live there with son or daughter, most likely in a room to the left (Allegany County Historian).

the head of household also occupied by his mother Sarah, age 50, and two younger children.

While over 90 percent of individuals living on the farm were members of the core nuclear family, it was common for a household to provide a home for needy relatives. As Table 4.6 shows, other household members tended to be older or younger dependent relatives. Occasionally a surviving aging parent moved in with son or daughter, or a needy brother, sister or grand child was taken into the farm home. An unmarried brother or sister of either the head of household or his wife sometimes lived and worked on the farm. It was not uncommon for a man to buy land in Allegany County, marry a local girl and provide a home for some of her dependent kin. Grandchildren were taken in when the child's parents died or were incapable of caring for the child. More rarely, outsiders were provided room and board in exchange for their labor. The loss of privacy, the complexity of managing social relations among unrelated people, and the additional consumption requirements apparently exceeded the value of diversity and the productive contribution of outsiders.

Table 4.7 shows that in 1855, 25–30 percent of heads of household had migrated directly from New England. They tended to be older men who had cut their farms out of the forest in the 1820s and 1830s. Younger heads of household who were recent migrants to Centerville had migrated from

Table 4.6. Non Nuclear Family Members, Centerville Households, 1855

Category	Number	%
Aging Parents	17	15
Brother or Sister of Head of Household or Wife	27	24
Other Relatives	6	14
Apprentice	5	4
Boarder	8	7
Hired Man	5	4
Total	113	99%

Source: Compiled by the author from typescript of 1855 Census for Centerville, Jean Lang Historical Collection, Alfred State College.

Hudson Valley counties. It was not unusual for an elderly Allegany County farmer to have been born on a farm in New England and as a young man forced to migrate to the Hudson Valley to clear a farm. Then he sold his improved land and purchased low cost unimproved land on the western New York frontier. For example, Daniel Baldwin was born in Connecticut in 1785 and lived in Connecticut in 1806 when his son Lewis was born. His second son was born in 1819 in Livingston County, adjacent to Allegany County, so we know that Daniel moved to Livingston County after 1806 and before 1819. Daniel moved on to Allen in 1825. At age 70 in 1855, he lived alone on his farmstead of 30 years, his wife Demaris having died. His son Lewis, age 49, and wife Catherine lived on a nearby farm with their five children ages eight to 17.

Fewer than 20 percent of heads of household were born locally, in Allegany or adjacent counties. Typically, these young men had either taken over the family farm from an aging father, or purchased unimproved land nearby and begun to clear a new farm. Many older sons, who could not expect to inherit the family farm anytime soon and confronting high land prices in the Centerville area where much land had already been cleared, migrated west.

Table 4.7. Reported Place of Birth, Heads of Household

Place of Birth	Allen		Centerville		Granger	
	N	%	N	%	N	%
New England	59	30%	76	29%	63	25%
Eastern New York counties	63	32%	85	33%	77	31%
Great Britain, Germany	22	11%	33	13%	49	19%
Counties bordering Allegany	16	8%	23	9%	26	10%
Allegany County	18	9%	27	10%	22	9%
Other states, unknown	18	9%	16	6%	14	6%
Total	196	99%	260	100%	251	100%

Many settlers who migrated to Allegany County in the 1830s and 1840s were born in England. They moved to late settled towns like Granger where abundant cheap land was still available.

By mid-century, the farm making process in Western New York was largely complete. Many hillside fields were converted from mixed subsistence crops to pasture land for dairy cattle. Farms increased in size and land prices rose from 1836 to 1855. A sample of 23 land transactions recorded in Belmont in 1836 and 19 in 1855 indicated that per acre price of land more than doubled from 1836 to 1855. In 1836, only four transactions were new farmers buying unimproved land at $2 per acre. The rest were settlers unloading their cleared land for two or three times what they had originally paid. As wheat and later dairy farming became established, land prices increased sharply to over $9 per acre in 1855.

CENTERS AND BACKWATERS: VARIATION AMONG TOWNS IN 1855

At mid-century, many farms were still largely self sufficient. Over one half of New York State farmers produced a surplus for market in 1855, and about two-thirds marketed goods in 1865 (Parkerson 1995). The 1855 census taker tells us how Allegany farm families earned their living, detailing the transition from logging to agriculture on many Allegany County farms. The speed of this transition varied from town to town. Towns settled earlier and having larger populations in the early settlement years were also the more advanced towns in 1855. With railroad and canal running through them, they enjoyed low transportation costs. In these towns, the shift to dairy production was well under way. They supported most of the 258 schools, 148 retail stores and 67 hotels and inns reported in the Allegany County census. In the less advanced towns, trees still covered the hill sides and populations were small. Hard pressed, recently arrived migrants were occupied in cutting the trees down and starting their farms on the cleared land.

Table 4.8 compares the value of agricultural and industrial production in the six wealthiest and the six least developed towns in 1855. How can we explain the success of the economic centers? All were located along the Genesee Valley Canal or the Erie Railroad and benefited from a decisive transportation cost advantage. Amity enjoyed the best water power location in the lower Genesee River. The census of 1855 contained data for 17 lumber mills located in the town of Amity. The mill of the Cooley family was one of the bigger operations in the township. With $6,000 invested in real estate and another $1000 invested in machinery, they had sales of

Table 4.8.   Value of Production, Twelve Allegany Towns, 1855

Economic Centers		Economic Backwaters	
Town	Value of Production	Town	Value of Production
Amity	$1,272,000	Willing	$256,000
Cuba	$1,069,000	Clarksville	$276,000
Wellsville	$962,000	Birdsall	$273,000
Almond	$882,000	Alma	$310,000
Belfast	$851,000	Grove	$323,000
Rushford	$819,000	Genesee	$347,000

Source: Calculated from town data on agriculture and manufacturing, 1855 Census

$179,480. They produced a staggering 17,500,000 board feet of lumber and 800,000 shingles. A skilled shingle maker cut 1000 shingles per day, reducing18-inch blocks of wood to half-inch shingles. The mill employed 25 men at an average monthly wage of 28 dollars a month. In 1849, the president of the Allegany County Agricultural Society complained that Cooley's ability to pay such high wages was driving up the cost of labor on local farms (McNall 1952, p. 194).

Cuba, Wellsville and Belfast villages were construction centers for the Erie Railroad and Genesee River Canal. Raw logs flowed into these villages from heavily wooded neighboring towns for export to Rochester and eastern urban markets. The towns of Almond and Rushford were still populous and wealthy, but they were on the decline owing to their now unfavorable location. Almond was located on the Erie Railroad, but fell under the lengthening shadow of Hornell and Wellsville. Rushford's strength earlier in the century was its relatively easy access to Buffalo by road, but the railroad eliminated that advantage. The population of Almond and Rushford declined by about 17 percent from 1855 to 1865.

Small manufacturing workshops were concentrated in the economic centers but were widely distributed throughout the county. For example, 23 grist mills were located in 16 different towns and 29 shingle makers worked in 13 towns. No town supported more than two grist mills or shingle makers. In 1855, transportation was still costly; local farmers continued to acquire important goods and services in the nearest village.

The value of cheese had tripled from 36 cents a pound in 1839 to one dollar a pound in 1859, reflecting increased demand for cheese among workers in eastern seaboard cities and in England. Young men who cleared the land eventually became the older men who operated dairy farms. The average years in residence for heads of household involved in cheese production was one-third longer than those not involved in dairy farming.

Blacksmith and carriage maker worked side by side in this salt box style workshop in Cuba. The blacksmith fashions wheels for the carriage maker. They mostly serve farmers who live within a four mile radius of their shops.

By 1855, the early settled towns of Alfred, Centerville and Cuba had moved from lumbering to specialized dairy production. Over 58 per cent of heads of household came to Alfred directly from the New England states or from New York counties in the Hudson and Susquehanna River valleys. The average farm in Alfred was made up of 65 acres of improved land and 33 acres of unimproved land. Seventy-one percent of the heads of household in the town were farmers. No lumber industry was in operation by 1855 because Alfred was settled early and the process of clearing the forest for pastureland or home building was completed. The settlers were now mostly growing crops and pasturing animals. Over 28 percent of Alfred farms were involved in cheese production. The average farm produced 2,424 lbs. of cheese, a per capita output of $102. The Erie Railroad transported the cheese to New York City. Alfred's highlands supported sheep farming more readily than crop production and the per capita output of wool was $16. The railroad transported wool to the large textile factories of Massachusetts.

By 1855, the average Centerville farm was made up of 64 acres of improved land and 34 acres of unimproved land. The average farm value was $2,067. About 18 percent of Centerville's initial immigrants came from nearby Rochester and Buffalo. Centerville also had the largest percentage of heads of household involved in farming at 87 percent. Nearly half of Centerville heads of household had been building their farms for over 21 years. Sim-

By mid century, farmers with substantial improved acreage had built barns to store hay and protect animals during the frozen winter months. Wagons would draw up to the platforms and the men would pitch the hay into the loft. The horses appear to be powering a grinding wheel (Allegany County Historian.)

ilar to Alfred in the progression from subsistence farming to more specialized agriculture, 23 percent of Centerville's farms were involved in dairy farming. Average cheese output was the highest of all townships at 3,507 lbs. The average number of cows on farms was the highest of all townships at six. Also by this time, the commercial lumber industry in Centerville had almost disappeared. The six small mills in the town produced less than $12,000 worth of output.

Cuba lies on the western border of the county and is drained primarily by Oil Creek, which connects with the Allegheny River at Olean. Oil Creek was a beginning point for the massive migration west at the early part of the nineteenth century. Travelers heading west would arrive in Cuba in anticipation of the spring floods. Raft building was a huge enterprise in Cuba during this time. The rafts were 16 to 24 feet in length and cost around two dollars per linear foot (Beers, 1978). They were said to hold five to six families as they descended down the Allegheny River to Pittsburgh and Ohio. The Allegheny also provided a great means of transport for getting lumber to market. Cuba's population grew as the migration west through the headwaters of the Allegheny continued.

Construction of railroad and canal in the 1850s increased the demand for labor and attracted immigrants from Europe. About 15 percent of Cuba's

This warehouse still stands along the Genesee Valley Canal site at Belfast. The cupola at the top afforded a view of traffic coming up and down the canal (author's photo.)

heads of household came directly from Europe. A comparatively small 55 percent of the heads of household were involved in farming. Large numbers of migrants passing through the town explains why four percent of heads of household were employed as merchants, the largest percentage in these six towns.

The average farm in Cuba consisted of 65 acres of improved land and 36 acres of unimproved land. Considering that Cuba was founded 10 years later than Alfred, one would expect less cleared land. This accelerated rate of clearing in Cuba is most likely a result of the demand for lumber by raft builders and railroad and canal construction. The business and trade that came together in Cuba where canal, railroad and traffic intersected supported a diversified economy. Cuba devoted 13 acres per farm to grain production, because a mill was built in 1822 in North Cuba. Prior to this mill being built, Olean and Angelica were the nearest places to have grain processed. In addition, a flat two-mile wide valley runs north/south through the center of Cuba township. Today, this valley contains some of the prime farmland in the county.

Amity, located in the Genesee River Valley, was settled in 1804. As in Alfred, a large percentage of the heads of household came here from the East Coast states and New York counties adjacent to the Susquehanna and Hudson River valleys. Forty-five percent of heads of household were farmers, compared to Alfred's 71 percent. Thirty percent of Amity's heads of household were employed as lumberman, laborers and carpenters. Amity's population, 1,485 in 1845, nearly doubled by 1855 to 2,655 (Beers, 1978). Labor was needed to build the Erie Railroad and the Genesee Valley Canal and to cut down trees for the booming lumber industry in 1855. Per capita lumber output was $226. The streams and creeks that flowed into the Genesee carried logs during spring high water levels to sawmills in the valley. The Genesee provided power to run these saw mills, and the Genesee Valley Canal provided the means to transport logs to support the large demand for lumber in the city of Rochester itself.

The economic backwaters in Table 4.8 above continued to be overwhelmed by their unfavorable topography and location. In these more remote, lightly populated towns, seasonal loggers cut trees and hauled the logs downhill on the frozen ground during the winter months. Lumbering was strong in the late-settled, lightly populated towns of Genesee and Bolivar, lumbering being the principal occupation of about 17 percent of the work force. Much lumber was used locally to house a growing population, and some was floated down the creeks to the Allegany River and on to Pittsburgh, which in 1850 was a rapidly growing city of 47,000. The transition from lumbering to dairy farming was complete by 1865, when fewer than two percent of Allegany County workers earned their living by cutting trees and sawing lumber (1865 New York State Census).

Bolivar, located in the southwestern corner of the county, was settled late, lightly populated, and economically impoverished. The average farm in Bolivar consisted of 22 improved and 72 unimproved acres. This 1:3 ratio of improved to unimproved acres was the largest among the townships, reflecting the late settlement date and the distance of the township from railroad and canal. Bolivar farmers devoted only five acres to grain, the lowest acreage in the six towns. At this time, acreage had not been cleared to make growing grain possible. Cuba had the nearest mill and farmers would put their grist on a sled drawn by oxen. The journey consumed two to three days (Beers, 1978).

The average cash value of farms in Bolivar was $1,410, the lowest of all townships. Bolivar had the largest percentage of heads of household involved in lumbering. The transition to agricultural output other than subsistence farming had barely begun. Bolivar had the highest percentage of log or shanty homes, 28 percent, in the county.

Few residents came to Bolivar directly from Europe because no industry was up and running and demand for laborers was low. The only industry data reported were six operations that involved lumbering, one cabinetmaker and a shoemaker. Workers in lumbering were paid a monthly wage of $18-$20, half of what the lumber mills in Amity were paying their employees. The per capita lumber output was $40 in Bolivar in 1855, compared to $400 in Amity. This low lumber output again points to Bolivar's isolation and lack of transportation. Only 10 percent of occupations in Bolivar were white collar merchants, clerks, clergy, doctors and other professionals. Doctors and school teachers had modest credentials in Bolivar in 1850; Bolivar's doctor, Joseph Cutler, was 23 years old. (Census records for Bolivar are available at the Bolivar Library.)

Grove, located in the northeastern corner of the county, was first settled in 1818. Only seven percent of heads of household had migrated to Grove from the distant Susquehanna River Valley. Over 80 percent of heads of household were farmers. The average farm was made up of 35 improved acres and 50 unimproved acres. The New York State Census for 1855 contained no records of industrial output.

Farmers in the township were active in grain production and its eleven acres per farm devoted to grain were second only to Cuba. Many farmers were still largely self-sufficient, while more prosperous farmers elsewhere in the county with better access to the railroad were specializing in dairy production. Grove did lead all townships in producing an average of 243 lbs. of maple sugar. Maple sugar was used as barter material and traded at local stores (Mau1958). The largest average maple sugar output among the six townships was in the poorest township, because the act of tapping trees and boiling sap required far less labor and capital than the production of cheese and dairy products.

About 40 percent of rural males between 18 and 35 fought for the north in the civil war (Denhom 2006 p. 109). Several thousand young Allegany County men out of a total county population of 40,000 left their fields to fight for the union in the Civil War, making labor scarce. Allegany County respondents reported that mean annual wages for farm labor in 1865 had increased 22 percent to $265, that farmlands had increased in value, and that farmers had reduced their debt load (New York State Census 1865). Sixty-two percent of Allegany County schools were classified as in good or very good condition, compared to 57 percent statewide.

Census takers in 1865 asked Allegany County respondents, "What changes in the social condition of the people have you observed since 1860? The census takers reported that, "At least nine-tenths speak cheerfully of the change which the war has wrought. The introduction of labor saving machines, the establishment of factories throughout the dairying sections for the making of cheese with great economy of labor. . ." Lampard 1963).

Statewide, New York had 61,500 more females than males in 1865, reflecting perhaps Civil War casualties and migration of males westward. But males exceeded females in Allegany and 16 other farming counties, mostly in the Southern Tier and Adirondack region. Life on the farm was hard, and a few women were beginning to take the train to the nearby village or city to seek their fortune. Some women preferred to remain unmarried, or married aging widowers whose farms were well established.

THE PROMISE OF AGRICULTURAL LIFE

Ebenezer Mix depicts the progress of the pioneer in towns like Alfred and Centerville after 45 years on the frontier. The settler has progressed from his assault on the dark forest to growing apples in his back yard, and from growing subsistence crops to specialized dairy farming. His log cabin has been replaced with a beautiful sawn-lumber home and farm outbuildings. Although not all homes looked like this by 1855, undoubtedly many did. A permanent bridge spans the creek, and the road leads to a prosperous village. He is shown holding the reigns of a sleigh, signifying his current prosperity (Mau 1958). Many agricultural innovations increased productivity.

By mid-century, transformation of the hillsides from forest to pasture had softened the farmer's attitude toward the world of nature. Fear and hostility

This engraving reveals a rather romanticized, positively cozy image of an early settler homestead. The farmer has successfully challenged nature, and shaped it to his purpose of providing for his family's material needs. This rendering of an 1855 farm was created in the late nineteenth century, when in the midst of the noise and grit of the early industrial revolution, people looked backward fondly to a simpler agrarian age. The picture conveys a sense of adequacy, comfort and control (Mau 1958.)

evolved into a romantic affection for the natural world. The Mix engraving conveys a sense of a landscape tamed and bestowing wealth and prosperity upon its human proprietors. The world of nature was no longer an opponent to be conquered but a cornucopia dispensing bounty to the diligent farmer.

The village of Philipsville, named after Philip Church, was renamed Belmont after the French "beautiful mountain," in the 1860s. As John M. Minard wrote, "Belmont is a beautiful name and no doubt was suggested for the village by the grand old hills in the neighborhood. . . . Gracefully receding from the widened river bottoms they ascend by easy gradations to heights majestic in their lofty attitudes" (Minard 1896, p. 446.) The Allegany County residents who read Minard's words readily appreciated his sentiment; their grandparents who originally settled the land had seen the dark forests as obstacles to growing crops, havens for menacing wolves and barriers to moving from farm to village.

People's affection for nature is also revealed in their incorporation of natural forms in the homes they built. Queen Anne homes feature irregular rooflines, complex window placements and multiple materials (wood, stone shingles, tiles) that echo the complexity of the natural landscape. Tastes in paint shifted from harsh whites to muted earth tones of grays, reds, browns and greens.

Classical builders had celebrated rational rules of balance and proportion to impose order on a disorderly natural world. This later Queen Anne in Angelica captures Romantic comfort with the natural world (author's photo).

Table 4.9.   Classification of Deaths, Allegany County, 1850

Age	Number of deaths	%
Under 1	1541	14.1%
1–5	2384	21.9%
5–under 10	707	6.5%
10–under 20	853	7.8%
20–under 50	2702	24.8%
50–under 80	2061	18.9%
Over 80	628	5.8%
Age unknown	25	.2%
Total	10,901	100.0%

Source: United States Census, State of New York Section, 1850.

As the post Civil War industrial revolution progressed, the beautiful rural landscape also came to represent the difference between urban and rural values. City populations grew quickly and extended urban political influence at the expense of rural populations. Cultural differences separated hard drinking Catholic immigrants in the cities and temperate, protestant native born farmers in the countryside. Rural dwellers came to believe that field and forest were closer to God than urban crowds and pavements. Face to face community bonds in rural New York softened the self interested impersonality of the commercial world. In the countryside, nature offered a retreat from the tensions of the commercial world.

The United States Census in 1850 collected information about mortality rates by county. Table 4.9 shows that in a population skewed toward young families, fully 36 percent of the deaths in 1850 were children under five years old.

If one lived to the age of five, early death was a continuing prospect. Nearly a quarter of deaths occurred among adults between ages 20 and 50, and apparently few farmers celebrated their 80th birthday.[3]

Most common causes of death were respiratory (consumption or tuberculosis and pneumonia), dysentery and various fevers. Only 87 women died in childbirth in 1850, compared to 232 people who died in accidents. Deaths were more common in winter and spring (59 percent) when short rations compromised the body's ability to fight off disease.

POLITICS AND THE CIVIL WAR

The issue of slavery transformed American party politics in the 1850s. Many Whig party voters bolted to the new Republican Party in the 1850s over the issue of slavery, setting up a long 150 year period in which a majority Republican Party and a minority Democratic Party competed in elections. In the rural north the strong anti slavery views of the new Republican Party appealed to Whig voters for whom the core of political life was promoting moral decency. Whig voters typically expected newcomers to their communities to value and practice hard working sobriety and protestant religion. They mistrusted non-English speaking immigrants. Democrats accepted the reality of cultural differences and adopted a live and let live attitude. That philosophy made sense to Irish Catholics in a New York City bar who were not morally offended by the economic institution of slavery and the racial attitudes of white southerners. The Whig Party quickly faded from the political scene, introducing a long period of competition between Republican and Democratic parties.

In Allegany County, Republican John Fremont won 72 percent of the vote in 1856, ushering in a long period of one party politics when the Republican Party typically won two thirds of the vote in national and state wide elections. On the brink of the slaveholders' rebellion, as the civil war was frequently called in Allegany County, Republican Abraham Lincoln won 72 percent of the presidential vote in Allegany County over Democrat Stephen Douglas. Table 4.10 shows the vote for president in 1860 in 29 Allegany County towns.

Lincoln carried all 29 Allegany County towns, but his margin of victory varied from town to town. In Allen, Centerville, Granger and Rushford, where pro-temperance farmers predominated, Lincoln won 90 percent of the vote. In Alma, Cuba, Scio and Wellsville, where more Irish laborers were working on railroad and canal construction, Lincoln received only 56 percent of the vote.

The complexity of Allegany County attitudes on the slavery question is captured in the recollections of famed abolitionist Frederick Douglass, who lectured in six Allegany County villages in October 1851. Douglass reports that audiences were generally sympathetic to his anti-slavery message. "To say that I am satisfied with my visit to Allegany County is but a feeble expression of my feelings," he writes. His message was most warmly received among farmers born in England, where the anti-slavery movement was more advanced, and among Seventh Day Baptists in Alfred and Nile.

However, Douglass was not particularly impressed with the level of interest and awareness of the Fugitive Slave Law and the anti-slavery movement among Allegany's hard working farmers. About 700 people usually heard the famed abolitionist speak at his lectures; the largest audience in Allegany County was 200. He encountered numerous proslavery people, including "the heartless proslavery principal of Friendship Academy" and a Presbyterian minister in Almond where "proslavery sectarianism was sufficiently strong to

Table 4.10.   Presidential Vote, 1860, 29 Towns

Town	Republican Vote	%	Democratic Vote	%
Angelica	278	75	90	25
Amity	352	70	151	30
Alfred	255	79	67	21
Almond	225	70	185	30
Allen	186	92	15	8
Alma	51	51	49	9
Andover	255	75	87	25
Belfast	284	76	92	24
Burns	193	83	39	17
Birdsall	92	61	89	8
Bolivar	156	70	68	30
Cuba	302	58	219	42
Clarksville	180	84	34	16
Caneadea	249	63	147	37
Centerville	252	86	40	14
Friendship	262	61	167	39
Genesee	198	84	38	16
Granger	220	93	31	7
Grove	107	60	71	40
Hume	349	77	104	23
Independence	224	77	66	23
New Hudson	216	76	67	24
Rushford	350	87	54	13
Scio	213	56	167	44
West Almond	136	72	3	28
Wellsville	286	59	199	41
Wirt	296	82	62	18
Willing	149	68	69	32
Ward	127	76	41	24
Total	6443	72	2530	28

Source: The Tribune Almanac and Political Register 1861, p. 43.

bolt the doors of a church against me." In Cuba, Douglass easily heard drinkers at the hotel saying, "That's the nigger that's going to lecture here tonight." (http://accesssible.palinet.org.scripts)

The transition from subsistence to cash crop farming was well under way in Allegany County by 1855. Population grew rapidly, meaning that more neighbors wished to exchange goods and services. Improved transportation dropped the cost of moving goods between city, village and farm. Farmers were eager to embrace new tools and techniques to enhance agricultural productivity. The village continued to grow as a center of commercial and manufacturing activity.

The Census of 1855 provides much detail about the migration patterns among western New York farmers, the size and composition of individual households and what the early farm house looked like. In 1855, the level of economic activity in towns varied widely. Economic centers typically were located in the river valleys where soils were fertile and access to low cost transportation readily available. In economic backwaters, small populations were still mainly engaged in lumbering activities, clearing the land. To the story of agricultural prosperity in Allegany County and western New York after the Civil War we now turn.

NOTES

1. Similar reasoning may explain why states began to extend to women the right to own property after 1850, a process that was completed by 1920. The property rights of women were strengthened earliest in those states that were urbanized and had high levels of economic development. Women had income earning opportunities but they would take advantage of them only if they could control their own earnings. Presumably, male legislators strengthened the rights of women to strengthen the incentive for women to work outside the home. Husband and wife become more like business partners, each contributing to the household's well being.

2. The 1840 census is by no means complete, and the 1855 census was the first attempt to collect information about economic activity at the county and town level. The data are known to be imperfect, especially in rural counties. Farmers and sawmill operators did not typically keep accurate records. Census takers had little instruction in how to record what they saw and what they were told. Some were more diligent than others. Mistakes occurred in Albany when clerks preparing the census deciphered wrinkled field notes written in eccentric hands. Not until the 1880 federal census had census taking practice evolved to the point where demographic and economic reality were recorded fairly accurately.

3. These figures are a profile of deaths that occurred in 1850 among a rather youthful population. These figures do not tell us the probability that a newborn child in 1850 will die before the age of one; we cannot infer that 14 percent of newborns will die before the age of one. Death did not rob families of their children at quite the rate these figures might suggest.

Chapter Five

Dairy Farming, Commerce and Rural Industry 1865–1900

The dairy industry in western New York evolved after the Civil War in response to changes in demand and supply for milk. On the demand side, more workers found employment in the growing cities of the Empire State. Worker families could buy more milk and cheese with higher wages in the post Civil War economic expansion. Nationwide, per capita consumption of cheese increased from 2.3 pounds per capita in 1880 to 3.9 pounds in 1910, about a 60 per cent increase (Lampard 1963). Large quantities of cheese were also exported to Europe. On the supply side, firm milk prices and technical advances in agriculture and animal husbandry enabled western New York farmers to increase production. Farm gate prices for cheese held steady at 8 to 12 cents per pound from 1875 to 1916. Dairy prices skyrocketed to 25 cents per pound during World War I because of strong wartime demand for condensed milk and prices remained strong during the 1920s.

DAIRY FARMING IN WESTERN NEW YORK

By 1865, cheese making was shifting from family farm to local factory. Labor saving mechanized cheese presses and skilled labor made factory production more efficient than individual farm production. Poor quality control was an inevitable feature of household production. In the absence of any reliable test for assessing the quality of the product, farmers were sorely tempted to dilute the milk they delivered. As one dairy industry watcher commented, "The most prosperous farmers do not dilute their milk with water. They dilute their water with milk" (Stamm 1991). The quality of milk and cheese improved dramatically with pasteurization and development of tests

Table 5.1.   Cheese Production in Allegany County, 1865–1975

Year	Number of factories	Production (m lbs.)	Production per factory (000 lbs.)
1865	6	1.2	500
1892	80	8.5	1000
1947	14	4.3	3000
1975	1	3.7	3700

Source: Stamm 1991

for bacteria count and butter content. Table 5.1 illustrates the rise and fall of factory cheese production in Allegany County.

With the advent of factory production, women lost control of the income from cheese making. Men transported milk to the factory, negotiated the price and handled the money. Respondents in 1865 who spoke cheerfully of "the change which the war has wrought" were males, who gained greater control of cheese making finances with the introduction of the factory system. The ethic of the family subsistence farm in which men and women were near equal in the household economy gave way to the idea that men were to bring home the money and women were to spend it caring for the children and managing the home (Cherlin 1996).

In the 1890s, farms typically milked 10–15 cows, the milk being made into cheese at 80 small factories located in all 29 Allegany towns. In the early 1900s, the worldwide price of cheddar cheese was set in weekly meetings in Cuba village. In several dozen villages across the county, business blocks built of durable brick sprang up, housing an array of businesses that catered to farm and village customers who had unprecedented sums of money to spend. Cheese production dominated the local economy.

However, Allegany County was hardly the center of cheese production in New York State. In 1860, New York State produced 46 percent of all cheese in America, and about 60 percent of New York cheese was produced in seven Mohawk and St. Lawrence River valley counties. Growing conditions for feed crops in these counties were more favorable, and they were closer to eastern urban and export markets.

With the railroad, farmers could ship their milk to eastern markets quickly and cheaply. However, Allegany County farmers were not the principal beneficiaries of lower transportation costs. The pricing policy of the Erie Railroad was to charge what the traffic would bear. Intense competition on the Chicago—New York route kept freight prices low. In the Southern Tier counties, the Erie had a transportation monopoly, allowing the company to charge western New York farmers high prices. For example, in 1857, railroads charged $35 per carload to transport livestock from Chicago to New York

Farmers in the Belmont area brought their milk to Borden's factory, where the milk was made into cheese and shipped to East coast and Erie Canal cities (Hinkle Library Alfred State College).

City. The Erie charged western New York farmers $85 per carload (McNall 1952, p. 237). In 1859, the Erie charged 62 cents per barrel to carry flour from St. Louis to New York City, and 65 cents to carry the same barrel of flour from Portageville to New York. Any advantage of proximity to eastern seaboard markets for western New York farmers over their Midwestern competitors was wiped out by this discriminatory railroad pricing (Benson 1955).

Very local geographic conditions influenced the timing and extent of change in dairy farming within Allegany County. Towns drained by the Susquehanna and Genesee Rivers, towns with lower average elevations and towns located closer to early nineteenth century trading centers were settled earlier and had larger populations in 1840 (Rasmussen 2001). These more heavily populated Allegany County towns along the Susquehanna and lower Genesee Rivers stripped their hills of lumber and moved into dairy production earlier than did more remote towns where settlers could not begin clearing the hills profitably until completion of the Erie Railroad and the Genesee Valley Canal in the early 1850s. The oldest towns in the Susquehanna River Valley were substantially out of lumbering by 1855. Here the transition to dairy was complete, and cows now grazed in the pastures that succeeded the original forest. Pasture land increased in value as dairy production became established.

The rise in farm value is apparent in the few cases where near identical pieces of land were sold. One 69 acre holding sold for $23 per acre in 1862 and for $37 per acre in 1875. A large 252 acre holding of unimproved land sold for $10 per acre in 1867; the same property doubled in value to $21 per acre in 1882. A 148 acre parcel in the town of Almond sold for $580 in 1840 and its value increased eight-fold in 40 years, selling for $5110 in 1883 (Allegany County Property Deeds, Belmont NY) .

A PORTRAIT OF TWO ALLEGANY TOWNS IN 1875

Now we turn to the impact on rural villages in western New York of agricultural, industrial and commercial growth, using materials found in commercial directories published in 1875 and 1905. These commercial directories provide detailed information about the economic structure of villages and the lives of village residents. Using these commercial directories, we can compare how social life was organized. The directories contain a wealth of useful information about local residents, including their names, gender, marital status, occupation, and size of land holdings. The town of Willing was settled late and was still in transition from logging to farming in 1875. The town of Rushford was settled early and its location in the fertile Genesee River Valley and along the Genesee Valley Canal assured its prosperity in 1875.

Table 5.2 shows some variation in size of Willing and Rushford farms in 1875. About one-fifth of farm households worked less than 40 acres. These small farms could not support a family, and most small land holders were retired or earned most of their income as cooper or physician, farming a bit on the side. Small 41 to 70 acre farms where households practiced mixed subsistence farming were much more common in Willing than Rushford. In Willing, only three farmers pastured dairy cattle in 1875. Larger farms over 121 acres were much

Table 5.2.   Farm Acreage, Town of Willing and Rushford, 1875

| | *Willing* | | *Rushford* | |
N Acres	N	%	N	%
Under 40 acre	38	19%	1	18%
41–70 acres	56	28%	36	16%
71–120 acres	64	32%	66	29%
Over 121 acres	41	21%	81	36%
Total	199	100%	224	100%

more common in Rushford, where the transition to dairy farming was complete. Each of six very large farms over 300 acres in Rushford were worked by two families, or part of the land was leased out.

In the town of Willing, industrial and commercial activity was limited in 1875, as shown in Table 5.3. Four out of five households practiced mixed farming, producing to meet household needs and perhaps marketing small surpluses. Only a handful of farms had shifted to dairy production. Local farmers supported relatively few blacksmiths, carpenters and storekeepers in the small villages of Shongo and Stannards. One man still earned his living as a "notion peddler," driving his wagon of useful household items from farm to farm. In 1875, a trip to town over rough, muddy roads was time consuming and hard on the family horse. The notion peddler provided a convenient, if costly, service to the farm household.

Table 5.3 shows that the economy of Rushford town was much more diversified in 1875 than was the Willing town economy. Early manufacturers included cheese factories (three), saw and shingle mills (four), and factories producing iron products, doors and windows and agricultural implements. Shops on the village of Rushford's Main Street offered such sophisticated services as jewelry sales, confectioner, drugs and stationary, fire and life insurance, a photographer, stage coach service to Cuba and Arcade, and a billiard parlor. The Willing directory listed 252 employed in 1875 of whom only 23 (10 percent) were employed in non farming occupations, primarily skilled craftsmen, business owners and school teachers.

During the 30 years from 1875 to 1905, the percent of the labor force employed in non-farming occupations tripled in the town of Willing (Table 5.4). The new petroleum industry employed dozens of oil field workers. Many new service providers lined Main Street in the villages of Shongo

Table 5.3. Occupations, Towns of Willing and Rushford, 1875

	Willing		Rushford	
Occupation	N	%	N	%
Farmers	199	79%	224	59%
Lumbering	9	4%	6	2%
Skilled craftsmen	9	4%	73	19%
Commercial businesses	7	3%	26	7%
White collar workers	7	3%	34	9%
Retirees, not in labor force	21	8%	17	4%
Total	252	101%	380	100%

Source: Hamilton Child, Gazetteer and Business Directory of Allegany County, N.Y. for 1875, Syracuse, 1875; Directory of Allegany County N.Y., 1905, Elmira, George Hanford, 1905.

In Belfast, the local bakery delivered its wares to your kitchen. Similar commercial services were not available in Willing in 1870 (Belfast Historical Society).

and Stannards, including a bicycle repairer, telephone lineman, butcher and dressmaker. Dairy farming was now firmly in place in Willing. Farmers were milking an average of 12 cows on 48 of 180 (27 percent) of farms. Farmers with small land holdings frequently leased land from a neighbor who had other employment or more land than he could comfortably farm. The number of households who earned their primary income from farming fell from 75 percent in 1875 to 57 percent in 1905 and only four households now earned income from logging related activities. Farm consolidation was underway; small farmers sold out and accepted the type of non-farming occupations listed in Table 5.4. The total number of farms had declined by 10 percent, but the number of large farms over 121 acres increased by 20 percent.

The number of farms in Rushford was identical in 1875 and 1905 but the number of large farms over 121 acres was greater in 1905. Of 224 farms in Rushford, 122 (54 percent) now specialized in dairy production with an average of 14 cows per farm. These farms were too large for a single family to work given the technology of the day. The number of farmers who leased the land they worked more than doubled to 53 in 1905 and in several cases, a father and son or two brothers operated a large farm jointly.

Table 5.4.   Non-Farming Occupations, 1905 for Willing and Rushford

	Willing		Rushford	
Occupation	N	%	N	%
Oil Field Workers	35	22%	—	—
Skilled craft workers	24	15%	52	36%
Commercial business	16	10%	29	20%
Laborers	45	28%	11	8%
Domestic workers	14	9%	4	3%
White collar workers	20	12%	43	30%
Other	7	4%	6	4%
Total	161	100%	145	101%

COMMERCIAL GROWTH IN FILLMORE AND WELLSVILLE

After the Civil War, America experienced a period of rapid industrial and commercial growth centered on the major cities along the Atlantic seaboard and the great lakes. In New York State, New York City and cities along the Hudson River and the Erie Canal grew rapidly. Increasing demand for grain and dairy products in these cities created agricultural prosperity in the western New York countryside. The process of integrating Allegany County farmers into the broader national economy continued. During one month in 1888, agricultural products were loaded onto 71 railroad cars at Fillmore, while one Hume hardware dealer received 35,000 lbs. of freight.

Farmers became increasingly committed to production for the market and spent their growing incomes on a cornucopia of attractively priced goods and services available in nearby villages. By the turn of the century, large factories employed dozens of workers on assembly lines replacing the small workshop that employed about four men that prevailed in 1855. Social life in these and other villages also changed between 1875 and 1905, a 30-year period of prosperity in Allegany County. The face of Main Street commercial shops changed, first with the appearance of the Montgomery Ward and Sears catalog and later as department stores replaced the old general stores on Main Street. The general store lost out because their prices were high and selection limited. Store keepers had to spread their fixed costs over a small sales volume, and could not earn volume discounts from suppliers.

The village of Fillmore provided the same staple goods and services in 1900 as had commercial enterprises in the village 50 years earlier, but the general store had now separated into several more specialized businesses. In 1900, prosperous cheese farmers with money to spend came to nearby villages like Fillmore to purchase more food and ready-made clothing; use the

Table 5.5.   Types of Businesses, Fillmore NY, 1900 (number)

Food and dry goods (3)	Drug store (2)	Hardware (1)
Furniture and undertaker (1)	Carriage maker (1)	Lumberyard (1)
Feed mill (1)	Hotels (3)	Insurance (1)
Newspaper (1)	Dress shops (2)	Blacksmiths (3)
Milliners (2)	Butchers (2)	

Source: *Latham's Village Directory 1900–1903*

services of dentist or blacksmith; get a haircut and visit the bank; buy useful items for home or barn at the hardware store. Clothing stores prospered, as few women had the time and talent to make clothes and trim hats at home. People owned more valuable homes and farms, and the new insurance industry enabled them to protect their property.

In 1900, traveling over bone-jarring, axle-breaking unpaved roads was still burdensome. Farmers were reluctant to wear out their horse and waste hours traveling to the nearest village and certainly not to the larger village farther away that might have a wider selection of goods at lower prices. On Saturday morning in 1900, about 50 teams crowded the streets of Fillmore as farm families ran errands and bought supplies. Of 330 Fillmore subscribers to Latham's, 41 were neighboring farmers. Stores listed in Table 5.5 provided

The well-stocked shelves of Fish and Crawford drug and grocery store in Belfast about 1925 (Belfast Historical Society).

the full range of goods and services available in many Allegany County villages at the time.

By 1888, railroad passenger service enabled rural villagers to travel conveniently to large villages and regional cities. Passenger trains ran three round trips daily to Rochester, and on weekends special excursion trains ran to area village fairs and to picnic areas at Letchworth Park and Silver Lake (Smith 1895). But travel by train was expensive. A round trip day long excursion to Niagara Falls cost $1.50. At the time, a worker in the local cheese box factory earned about $1.00 a day. So that trip to Niagara Falls cost our young worker and his girl friend about three days' wages. Today, a minimum wage worker will earn in one hour what an early industrial worker earned in a week. A couple would drive their car to Niagara Falls at a cost of perhaps $20—about three hours' wages.

A few strategically located regional villages like Wellsville, Hornell, and Arcade expanded in size, but small villages like Fillmore, Rushford and Whitesville could not support larger and more specialized stores. Being on the Erie Railroad gave Wellsville and Hornell an economic advantage over Friendship and Canaseraga. Consumers in small villages took horse and wagon to the nearest train station, traveled to Wellsville to purchase a cook stove, bed frame and new clothes, and returned late in the day.

Penn. R. R. Station, Belfast, N. Y.

The train expanded the horizons of western New York villagers. These Belfast area residents took excursions to Letchworth Park or to the village of Wellsville or simply dressed up to meet the train in their finest garb (Allegany County Historian).

Table 5.6. Types of Businesses, Wellsville NY, 1900

Retail Sales	*Services*
Department store (2)	Insurance (3)
Clothing store (3)	Bank (2)
General store (3)	Newspaper (5)
Shoe store (6)	Church (10)
Meat market (4)	Restaurant (2)
Bakery (4)	Hotel (3)
Stationer (2)	Saloon (4)
News and tobacco (2)	Billiard parlor (1)
Florist (1)	Barber (6)
Confectioner (2)	Laundry (1)
Jeweler (2)	Livery (1)
Furniture	Undertaker (1)
Hardware store (3)	Photographer (1)
Lumber dealer (2)	
Bicycle dealer (1)	*Small manufacturers*
Music store (1)	Oilfield supply (1)
	Tannery (1)
Public Utilities	Cigar maker (1)
Post Office (1)	Bottler (2)
Library (1)	Carriage maker (1)
Electric (1)	*Transportation*
Natural gas (1)	Railroad (2)
Water (1)	Stage coach (3)
	Delivery service (2)

Source: Collected from Latham's Village Directory 1900–1903

The village of Wellsville emerged as a major commercial center by 1900 experiencing a rapid period of growth after construction of the Erie and Pittsburgh Shawmut and Northern railroads that intersected at Wellsville. Stage coach services connected neighboring villages with the Wellsville hub. Stagecoaches left Bolivar daily at 7:00 a.m. for the three and a half hour trip to Wellsville. The traveler had four hours before the return stage to Bolivar departed. Some travelers stayed the night at the hotel or with friends and family. By 1900, Wellsville had established itself as a dominant economic center in the regional economy with 10 percent of the total county population. Before the arrival of the railroad in 1855, at least six villages (Angelica, Almond, Belmont, Cuba, Friendship and Rushford) had exceeded Wellsville in size. In 1843, eight of Allegany County's 45 post offices did a larger volume of business than Wellsville (Petri 1960).

Latham's Village Directory reveals that a richer array of goods and services was available in Wellsville than in villages closer to the shopper's home.

Downtown Wellsville about 1915, rapidly becoming the commercial center for Southern Allegany County. The brick business block has replaced the original wooden buildings. Horse and buggy and new Model Ts share the street and electricity is installed (Allegany County Historian).

As a store in Wellsville could spread their fixed advertising, insurance and record keeping costs over a larger sales volume, they could charge less for a yard of cloth or a pound of coffee than could the shopkeeper in Hume or Canaseraga. Also, market place competition gave the Wellsville shopkeeper an incentive to provide their customers with the best service and the lowest price. Table 5.6 shows that buyers in Wellsville could choose among three hardware stores, four meat markets, three drug stores and six shoe stores. The smaller village of Fillmore had only one or two of each. A larger village also supported specialty stores such as a billiard parlor, music store, two jewelers, a florist and a furniture store. When Scio residents craved chocolate or needed a bicycle, they traveled to Wellsville.

FARMERS AND VILLAGE MERCHANTS:
ANOTHER PRISONER'S DILEMMA GAME

Over the decades, local farmers as buyers and village merchants as sellers had worked out their Prisoner's Dilemma game in various ways. Although buyers and sellers were natural adversaries, each had an interest in developing stable relationship that recognized the essential interest of each. Merchants extended credit and accepted the farmer's surplus in trade. Farmers made payments on their debt as they could. At best, the ongoing interaction between store owner and farmer over the years was the basis for a personal relationship based on trust, cooperation and reciprocity (3,3). Of course, each player was tempted to defect. The store owner was tempted to overcharge and to ignore complaints in search of greater profit (4) in the short run at the expense of his customers (1). That strategy was risky in that a rival might open a competing store, or the farmer might drive his wagon to the slightly more distant town in the other direction from his farm gate. Farmers were equally tempted to take advantage of the storekeeper by neglecting to make timely payments on his debt or shoplifting, or taking his business elsewhere.

In the 1890s, farmers did desert the small village general store in favor of Richard Sears' mail order catalog. Sears worked to build a long term relationship with his rural customers, offering money back guarantees, free delivery and the convenience of collect on delivery (COD) payment. "Honesty is the best policy," said Sears. "I know because I've tried it both ways." (Weil 1977 p. 25). Sears established a loyal customer base in rural America (3,3). Local shopkeepers fought back unsuccessfully, offering discounts to customers who would turn in their Sears catalog and pressuring local newspapers not to carry Sears advertising (Emmett and Jeuck 1950, p. 18).

By 1897, the Sears catalog offered over 6000 items for sale in its 770-page catalog. Farm families could buy clothing, patent medicines, household goods, tools, sporting goods, and personal luxuries. Customers could join their neighbors to save more by buying in large quantities. Catalog shopping offered the convenience of ordering from one's own living room and the knowledge that Sears guaranteed their customer's satisfaction (Israel 1968). Sears bought large quantities of quality merchandise from suppliers all over the United States who shipped their goods to Sears' six-story warehouse in Chicago where 600 employees filled orders from customers. Sears was the "cheapest supply house on earth" because it could guarantee strong sales volume to suppliers in exchange for discounted prices.

Prices were lower in 1897 than they are today, but earning power was lower too. Table 5.7 compares the real cost to consumers of a market basket of goods selected from the 1897 Sears catalog and large store prices in 2006.

This selected market basket of items cost from 11 to 42 times more today than 100 years ago. In most cases, the consumer much prefers today's product to the Sears catalog offering. Yesterday's heavy wooden extension ladder is made from lightweight aluminum today, and today's automatic self cleaning electric range is a much better product than the Sears wood burning cook stove in 1897.

Table 5.7. Consumer Prices, 1897 and 2006

Consumer Item	Sears 1897 Catalog price	Retail Price 2006	Price Increase 1897–2006
Coffee (1 lb)	35 cents	$3.87	11 X
Flour (1 lb)	3 cents	35 cents	12 X
Baseball bat	75 cents	$18	24 X
Child's wagon	$1.30	$35	27 X
Webster dictionary	$1.68	$24	14 X
Woman's dress suit	$5.50	$72	13 X
Carpet (sq yd)	35 cents	$9	26 X
Cook stove	$13	$350	27 X
Extension ladder	$1.90	$80	42 X

Source: Fred L. Israel, 1897 Sears Roebuck Catalog; author's survey of large retail stores, August 7, 2006.

Today's median income family earns about $52,000, or about $208 per day. After deductions, disposable income is perhaps half, or about $104 per day. The median income in 1897 was about $1 per day, and no money was withheld for taxes. Therefore, to buy a pound of coffee required about three hours work in 1897, less than 20 minutes in 2006.

Sears in turn was challenged by the department store located in larger regional villages. They could match Sears prices and selection, and customers could see and touch the goods they were about to buy. Improved roads made travel easier, and the village drew customers from a wider radius.

MAINTAINING COMMUNITY VALUES

Social life in the villages of western New York was elaborate, strengthening ties among neighbors and defending standards of right behavior within the community. Parades were festive occasions that brought farm families into the village to visit and shop.

Fraternal orders, fire companies, baseball clubs, local bands provided opportunities for villagers to meet regularly, to reinforce community moral orthodoxy, and to sanction wrong doers. Many villages had an opera house or community theater, where traveling groups put on shows and local groups sponsored nights of entertainment.

Young men played baseball and participated in the village band. A purpose of these activities, in addition to having a good time, was to reinforce among young men the values of politeness, civility and acceptance of common rules of behavior. Those who engaged in rowdy behavior or failed to follow accepted rules of courting young women risked being ostracized.

Parades on national holidays and local occasions were a regular feature of life in small towns. Spectators wearing their finery line both sides of the street enjoying this 1907 parade in Rushford (Allegany County Historian).

In western New York, the Grange primarily served as a social fraternity for farm folk; nationally, the Grange sought to defend the interests of American farmers following the economic depression of 1873. In Allegany County, 24 of the 26 Grange branches were formed after 1904 (Allen 1934). The Grange sought to preserve the traditional way of life, including solidarity with neighbors, preserving a broad crop base, and minimizing dependence on debt producing machinery-even as farmers were steadily more integrated into the cash economy (Summerhill 2005, p. 170). The Grange provided an opportunity to alleviate isolation and the drudgery of rural life (Nordin 1974, p. 109). Grangers discussed how to stop marginal farmers from selling out and moving to town, how to improve the quality of farm life, and how to promote traditional family values. They formed farmer's cooperatives to purchase supplies and promoted agricultural extension education.

Grange members were farmers and their families, and fraternal rites and secrecy promoted solidarity among members. Grange rituals promoted recognition of women's contributions to the household economy and their role in promoting values of temperance and hard work. Women held important positions within national, state and local Grange branches. Their influence is apparent in the Grange positions on two major early twentieth century political issues, temperance and the extension of the franchise to

Social life in turn of the century villages was well developed, especially for young men who enjoyed more opportunities than did young women. These young men in the cornet band marched in parades and played in the village theater. Baseball teams in many villages played each other during the summer.

women (Allen 1934). Alarmed that their husbands and sons would succumb to the temptations of liquor and raucous behavior, women led the fight to curb the evils of alcohol in their community. The Women's Christian Temperance Union (WCTU) presented their case effectively in rural counties. The WCTU was instrumental in securing passage of the 18th amendment to the Constitution in 1919 that banned the manufacture and sale of alcoholic beverages.

Local community elites played an important part in defining orthodox behavior, praising conformity to social norms, and ostracizing those who strayed. These values were generally accepted among those who worked and shopped in the community and attended one of the churches. Beers' 1896 centennial history, *Allegany County and its People*, celebrates the achievements of successful families in the 29 towns. These original settlers and their contemporary descendants, who are prominent citizens, enjoyed economic success, fought for their country in the Civil War, and served the community in political positions, churches and social clubs. Thumbnail sketches of 30–50 successful families emphasize the family contributions over three generations (Minard 1896).

Rushford residents in 1890 remembering their male and female ancestors had very different standards for praiseworthy behavior in men and women.

These well established, serious minded women are attending a Women's Christian Temperance Union meeting in Cuba about 1910. These pillars of the social order blamed alcohol for all kinds of sexual license and anti-family behavior (Allegany County Historian).

Men are celebrated for their contribution to local prosperity, steadfast religious life, interest in local public affairs, and hard working habits. The community is their stage. Women are remembered for being helpful to others in need and for their social graces. The home is their platform (Merrill 1908.)

These admirable qualities of community leaders served to underline that many community members and less rooted travelers passing through town had no particular incentive to abide by community moral standards. They would rather drink on Saturday night than attend church on Sunday morning. Traveling salesman visiting Wellsville or Cuba for two days had no prospects for being accepted into a suspicious community.

Single men who resided in boarding houses and commercial travelers who stayed in a village for a few days were enthusiastic patrons of bars in Wellsville's three hotels and four saloons. Established community members particularly feared and disliked itinerant workers without ongoing community ties. Along Jockey Street in Belfast, canal boaters who stayed in town over the winter months raced horses, supported brothels, drank and fought through the 1860s. In the 1850s, itinerant wage workers who were building canal and railroad were known for their hard drinking and hard living behaviors during their short stay in a community. Oil field workers in Bolivar and Richburg

LOBBY OF NEW FRIENDSHIP
HOTEL, FRIENDSHIP, N. Y.

Every village on the line of rail had a hotel to serve commercial travelers. The lobby of the New Friendship Hotel in 1911 features comfortable leather rockers. Cigars and other goods are available at the front desk. Local residents viewed commercial travelers with suspicion (Allegany County Historian).

built their social life around saloons and bawdy houses in the 1880s, not the local churches.

In the village of Angelica, an abandoned foundry served as a "community flophouse for homeless drunks" and a meeting place for "unsavory characters." After numerous requests to the owner to tear down the building were ignored, local residents with heavy house moving equipment razed the building in the dead of night in less than two hours, the destruction being credited to a mysterious hurricane (Harry Gardner, *Angelica Collecteana*, p.14, unpublished manuscript, Angelica Public Library).

Following the logic of the Prisoner's Dilemma, it is easy to see why itinerant workers and settled villagers have a difficult time building relationships of cooperation and mutual trust (3, 3). They do not have a long future together because itinerant travelers are here today and gone tomorrow. In a single play game, each actor's best move is to defect, in which case the best possible outcome is (2, 2). Villagers have no reason to welcome travelers passing through the village and travelers have no reason to win approval in the village they are passing through. If either player generously cooperates, the other player is likely to take advantage and score four points over the cooperating sucker who earns one point.

WOMEN'S ROLE AS MANAGER OF THE HOME

Women organized the social life of the family. The woman of the house was expected to provide a pleasant place of refuge for her husband upon his return from the challenges of business and community affairs. She also had primary responsibility for the education and moral development of their children. She structured the family's social life. As an expert in home management, she had a position of power within the family (Baker 1991).

But the home was also a trap. Western New York farm women in 1840 had been full partners in generating the resources that supported the family. Two generations later, by 1880, the male head of household brought home the resources that supported the family, and the female's role was to manage the household (Clark 1986). The kitchen band enabled women to expand their activities beyond the house in a socially acceptable way.

Economic prosperity shaped popular ideas about housing and about the role of the woman in managing the home. Building a substantial house that reflected contemporary fashion indicated that the owner was economically successful and underlined the family's standing in the community. Stylish Italianate and Queen Anne homes indicated the material prosperity of the

The Little Genesee Kitchen Band played a variety of kazoos and homemade instruments. They performed in local village opera houses, traveling by trolley to Bolivar and Ceres to showcase their talent (Bolivar Library).

individuals who were able to build them. Large homes were an important indicator of economic success in an age when most opportunities for conspicuous consumption were connected to the home. Economic prosperity also meant that houses needed to be larger. More consumer goods and household conveniences were available, requiring more room for display and storage space.

Families increasingly valued privacy. Children needed separate rooms for sleeping, daily activities and storage of personal books, toys and belongings. At the very least, boy and girl children needed separate rooms. If an aging parent lived with a family, he or she needed private space of her own. By 1890, three-quarters of farm families in New York owned their own home (Census of the United States, 1930). However, as low-cost home mortgages were not generally available until the 1900s, home ownership was beyond the reach of the average American citizen. Large homes sometimes sheltered people who were not part of the nuclear family. A grandparent or needy youthful relation, a servant, and perhaps a boarder would occupy the space in a large Victorian home. Women in more prosperous households were able to hire household servants. In 1870, about one in eight families hired household servants, and half of all female wage earners were domestic servants (Clifford 1986).

With economic prosperity, tastes in domestic architecture changed dramatically. Italianate style evolved into more complex Victorian styles, which prevailed from 1870 to 1900. Around 1870, English and American travelers discovered Paris, a city dominated by the Mansard roof with its characteristic curved lower slope punctuated by dormers. Owners frequently modernized their Italianate homes by adding a Mansard roof to accommodate an additional story. Mansard roofs were made of various materials, including slate and multicolored tiles.

Queen Anne, or Victorian, houses express the confidence that small town communities would fully participate in the fast expanding industrial revolution that was ushering in a long period of wealth and prosperity. Queen Anne refers to the English label for early eighteenth century manor houses, during the reign of Queen Anne. The large homes that we know as Queen Anne did not really resemble their English namesakes in style, but they did in terms of visual and social importance in the community. Since paint manufacturers could now produce colors consistently, homeowners were able to use multiple shades of brown, green, red and gray. They combined these soft, earth tone colors in four color paint schemes.

Inside the Victorian home, space was devoted to specialized functions as reception hall, sewing room, bathroom and study. Family members could take advantage of various nooks and crannies, such as window seats and second

This colorful Mansard roof adorns a home on Main Street in Wellsville (author's photo).

This Queen Anne in Belmont shows the irregular roof line, multicolor painting scheme, different size windows and large porch for visiting on summer evenings. The building is now divided into apartments (author's photo).

floor balconies, to enjoy moments of privacy. Rooms contained ample shelves, cabinets and tables to show off Victorian bric a brac that demonstrated the family's taste and prosperity (McMurry 1988).

During this period of commercial and industrial expansion, some women continued to leave the family farm to seek their fortune in the village. The energy, excitement, and opportunity of life in Wellsville appealed to many young women growing up on Allegany County farms. Some preferred their life chances in the village to the physical rigors of life on the farm. Jobs for young woman were increasingly available in the villages, and some women preferred to marry a villager than to marry the boy who inherited the farm next door.

The directories suggest that nineteenth century women earned their status through marriage. It was not common in 1875 for women to work outside the home for wages. Women who worked in the home and were married usually did not have their name listed in the directory; when their husband died, frequently women were then listed as widows. Only 17 women (about six percent of the female population) were listed in the Willing Directory for 1875; all were widowed or single and about half worked outside the home as teachers or seamstresses. Several listed as farmers were widows who leased their acreage to a neighbor or male relative. Thirty years later, 86 women (19 percent of the female population) were listed in the Willing directory. About one-third worked as teachers, needle workers or domestic help. By 1905, 117 women in Rushford were listed. Over half were widows, and most of these owned property in their own names after the death of their husbands. Only 25 of these women (21 percent) were employed outside the home, almost all as teachers or in the needle trades.

Most women in turn-of-the-century Wellsville worked as home makers; the occupants of their home frequently included unmarried adult children or boarders, as well as husband and dependent children. *Latham's Directory* lists about 2,900 adults living in Wellsville in 1900, and 241, or about 17 percent of adult women, were employed in the market economy. Contrary to the picture of Victorian era women staying at home to manage the household, *Latham's Directory* shows that many women in turn of the century Wellsville also earned cash income on behalf of the household.

Table 5.8 shows that many women worked as domestics in boarding houses and in the homes of their wealthy neighbors, or they made dresses or fashioned hats. Made-to-order clothing available at Wellsville's two department stores, Rockwell's and Allen's Bargain Store, had not yet displaced the home based needle trades. Many teachers taught music to middle class children, working out of their home. Women were also employed as sales clerks in the 75 stores located in the Main Street business district, and women were

Table 5.8.   Female Occupations, Wellsville NY, 1900

Occupation	N	%
Needle Trades	62	25.7
Domestic Service	62	25.7
Teacher	44	18.3
Sales Clerk	23	9.6
Office Work	22	9.1
Other	28	11.6
Total	241	100.0

rapidly establishing a foothold in bookkeeping and secretarial work. Other occupations in Table 5.8 include cooking in the hotel restaurant, cigar making and providing nursing care.

MANUFACTURING IN WESTERN NEW YORK VILLAGES

As the industrial and commercial revolution deepened around the turn-of-the-century, most western New York villages sought to attract manufacturing enterprises that would provide jobs for local workers and generate increased sales for local businesses. Local communities had often subsidized the cost of starting a new business. In the 1860s, local communities sold bonds to support the construction of railroads connecting their village with a neighboring village, in the hope that both would prosper from reduced transportation costs and the ability to support new businesses. In the fast changing economy of the industrial revolution, many enterprises were started but few lasted more than 20 years. Successful plants were located near their customers, which favored urban locations, or near the raw materials that went into the product. The Alfred Celadon Tile Factory, for example, was developed adjacent to the clay deposits that were made into terra cotta roofing and decorative tiles.

The story of the Tanner Brothers Canning Factory in Belfast, 1897–1910, illustrates how difficult it was for a small village to attract and retain a manufacturing enterprise. The Tanner brothers asked the people of Belfast to purchase the land, upgrade the water supply, and construct the basic building. They did so. From the beginning, the Belfast canning factory struggled to collect the labor and raw materials needed to operate efficiently. The Genesee Valley could not produce enough fruits and vegetables to operate the factory at full capacity. Company representatives traveled throughout western New York to purchase the peas, beans, and apples that filled Tanner Brothers' cans.

Many western New York villages had a small factory, like the Empire Sash and Door Company in Friendship that processed local raw materials, employed one or two dozen workers, and supplied regional markets. Most were not very profitable and did not survive disasters like fire or economic recession (Hinkle Library, Alfred State College).

Since canning is a seasonal industry, many workers were women, who were more willing to be employed seasonally than their men folk who were at work in the fields. During the peak canning season, Tanner Brothers employed 100 hands, importing 40–60 Polish women from Buffalo to fill their quota of needed workers. The company housed these temporary workers in make-shift barracks.

In 1907, Tanner Brothers announced plans to relocate their plant to a Genesee County location where the firm was closer to a large supply of vegetables and fruits and closer to Buffalo's labor supply. Also, low cost electric power was available from the new Niagara Falls hydroelectric plant, and the factory's canned goods were closer to large markets in Buffalo and Rochester (*History of Tanner Brothers Canning Factory,* nd. Belfast Historical Society. Thanks to Mary Nangle for making this document available).

Development of the huge Pennsylvania oil field in the 1870s opened up the possibility that oil, not coal, would power the industrial revolution. Over 300 million years ago, great swamps covered northern Pennsylvania and western New York. The organic material in these ancient swamps was covered over with heavy sediments that became sandstone bedrock. Under great pressure

The Tanner Brothers Plant in Belfast which canned fruits and vegetables from 1897–1910 (Belfast Historical Society).

This machine shop in Bolivar provided tools used in the oil fields (Bolivar Library).

from the weight of this bedrock, the ancient organic material was transformed into pockets of coal and oil.

Oil was discovered in Allegany County at Richburg in April 1881 and within months some 8,000 men poured into the village to work in the oil fields. A shabby boom town of rooming houses, saloons and brothels sprang up over night and disappeared as quickly within a year when the floating population of oil field workers moved on to a new oil field in the Titusville, Pennsylvania area. Production fell from nearly seven million barrels in 1882 and stabilized at over one million barrels per year over the next 20 years (New York State Department of Environmental Conservation, Division of Mineral Resources).

Annual production exceeded two million barrels per year and peaked at over five million barrels per year during World War II. The introduction of water flooding (oil floats on water, bringing the oil closer to the surface) increased recovery rates. Demand increased as the tractor replaced the horse on western New York farms, automobile sales increased rapidly in rural areas, and oil began to replace coal for home heating after the war. For decades, Wellsville provided legal, banking and insurance and oil field services to the industry, and the stately homes that line Main Street in Wellsville testify eloquently to the contribution of oil to Wellsville's prosperity during the oil era,

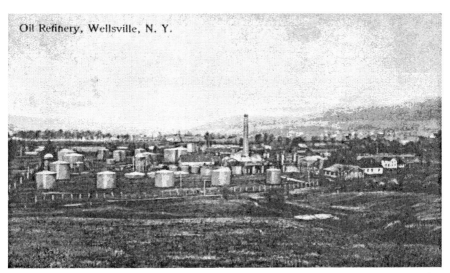

The Sinclair Oil Company opened an important oil refinery about 1895 and continued to refine oil there until 1954 (Allegany County Historian).

1881–1968. Table 5.4 above shows that in 1905 over one-fifth of Willing's non agricultural work force consisted of oil field workers.

The Sinclair Oil Company opened an important oil refinery in Wellsville about 1895 and continued to refine oil there until 1954. After 1968, oil production slumped to an average of one million barrels per day until about 1990, when the wells were capped. High recovery costs at Allegany County's oil wells, increasing global oil production, and falling real oil prices during the 1990s have stilled the oil pumps that rest along county roads.

POLITICAL PARTY COMPETITION:
RUM, ROMANISM AND REBELLION

Do economic class interests or cultural differences better explain political party competition between Republicans and Democrats after the Civil War? In terms of economic interests, the owners of banks and businesses and independent professionals may view the political world differently than do blue collar workers. More successful farmers may vote differently than small farmers struggling to survive (Burnham, 1981; Humphrey 2004). However, in rural western New York, economic factors like income or occupation do not predict very well whether a voter pulls a Republican or Democratic lever at the polls. Bankers and small business owners are only slightly more likely than wage earners to vote Republican. Low income farmers were no more likely to vote Democratic than higher income farmers.

Ethnic and cultural differences might better explain political identification (Benson 1961; Kleppner 1970). It seems likely that Republican prominence in the rural north after 1856 over the slavery issue was due less to the economic interest in slave labor versus free labor as in the moral conviction that slavery was wrong (Kleppner 1981, p. 118). After the Civil War, moral issues continued to dominate party politics. Local Republicans believed fervently in promoting right moral behavior. Their suspicion of alcohol drinking, Catholic, non-English speaking foreigners was deep. Democrats tended to accept ethnic and moral diversity and certainly rejected the idea that government should impose the moral values of the majority on everyone. The electoral base of the national Democratic Party was among immigrant workers in eastern and Midwestern cities and in the South, where white voters hated the civil war legacy of Republican Abraham Lincoln.

In Allegany County after the Civil War, the new Republican Party dominated its Democratic rival. Democrats were tarred as the party of "Rum, Romanism and Rebellion," a reference to hard-drinking Roman Catholic down state immigrants as well as Southern resistance to reconstruction after the

Civil War. In the 1867 election for governor, for example, the Republican candidate carried all 29 Allegany County towns and won 71 percent of the total vote. The towns of Allen, Centerville, Granger and Rushford cast 89 percent of their votes for Republicans. Only 56 percent of voters in Alma, Cuba, Scio and Wellsville supported the Republican candidate. Alma was a lightly populated lumbering town with few social institutions that promoted Republican moral values. The other more urban railroad towns had a more diversified population with larger numbers of Irish Catholic and German voters.

How seriously do people take their cultural differences as they play the political game? Fortunately, cultural conflict in western New York has not taken the form of a dominant culture seeking to destroy a minority culture (4,1). More common is a low grade animosity taking the form of cultural isolation, a nosy critical interest in other people's affairs, and flaunting cultural differences (2, 2). The more positive alternative is when players have face to face contact on a daily basis, adopt a live-and-let-live attitude, and reinforce shared values rather than dwell upon their cultural differences (3, 3).

Dairy farming was the engine of prosperity in Allegany County from 1865 to 1900. Farmers sold their milk to cheese making factories and spent their money purchasing the expanded array of goods available at the village general store. Later, Sears catalog and local department store made more goods available at affordable prices. Small factories converted milk into cheese, lumber into cabinets and furniture, and hides into leather. Prosperous villagers built larger homes in the latest style.

Men were the principal breadwinners, and women were increasingly seen as managers of the home, organizers of family social life and defender of community moral values. By the turn of the century, economic conditions were worsening for western New York farmers as dairy production in the Midwestern states expanded in the 1920s and demand for dairy products fell during the Great Depression. Village business felt the pinch as farmers had fewer dollars to spend. Local factories felt the competitive pressures from large urban factories that enjoyed greater specialization and economies of scale and therefore lower costs of production. In the 1920s, the new automobile and improved roads reduced transportation costs and transformed economic and social life. How would local communities that had been built around the railroad adapt to the automobile? To that story we now turn.

The Automobile and Rural Decline: 1900–1950

Although the years from 1900 through World War I were a period of agricultural prosperity in western New York, many rural people were leaving the farm for nearby village and regional cities. Catalogs and village stores reminded farmers that a cornucopia of products was available to families with larger incomes. The price of farm commodities was not keeping pace with higher prices for urban manufactured products, and hard pressed farmers concluded that they could earn more money in urban factories and commercial businesses. Young people especially felt the lure of the village, where employment opportunities and more varied alternatives to the intimacy of life in the farm house beckoned.

QUALITY OF RURAL LIFE

Rural populations were also pushed off the farm by the perceived shortcomings in rural life. The nineteenth century farm family had cultivated a network of social relationships with friends and neighbors. Helping your neighbor in time of need established the expectation that help would be reciprocated in turn. When cash was hard to come by, neighbors could provide help in time of need and companionship to alleviate loneliness and isolation of farm life. By 1900, farmers typically sold their dairy products on the market in exchange for cash, and traditional ties between neighbors were harder to maintain. A farmer could devote hours to helping a neighbor only at the expense of not getting his own work done and earning less from the sale of his milk. In a market oriented world, greater social distance, more privacy and less interaction tended to replace mutual help. More prosperous farmers who could take advantage of market opportunities were more inclined to loosen ties to neighbors than were more traditional farmers whose wealth lay in close, dependable relations with neighbors.

Another perceived shortcoming of rural life was that farmers needed to hire labor in peak seasons, and the burden of providing room and board fell heavily upon the women (Bowers 1974, p. 118). In terms of the Prisoner's Dilemma, a woman was less able to forge a cooperative relationship with hired help than with her own children. Hired field help tended to be unmarried men working seasonally who felt entitled to press for better room and board conditions, and women resented the extra work for an unappreciative audience (2,2). Relations based on civility and mutual consideration (3, 3) were less likely to develop in this arms length, impersonal relationship (Summerhill, 2005, p. 160). Close ties with neighbors weakened as farms relied more heavily on wage labor rather than traditional work sharing, and small neighbors sold out and moved away.

Efforts to improve the quality of rural life, like the Country Life Movement that flourished between 1900 and 1920, had two goals. One goal was to close the widening income gap between rural and urban people by increasing productivity on the farm. By investing in the latest agricultural technology and increasing the size of their holdings, farmers could enjoy the same material standard of living as urban dwellers. More progressive farmers purchased land from their less successful neighbors.

Local farmers with their hay wagons wait at the railroad station in Fillmore. Allegany County was a net importer of hay, and generally hay will be off loaded from the railroad cars to the farmers' wagons. But in this case, hay grown in the rich bottom lands of the Genesee River Valley will be exported to Rochester to feed horses hauling loads on the city streets (Allegany County Historian).

Many farmers, especially those farming less fertile hillside lands, were quite critical of the patronizing efforts of urban reformers to transform farm life. Buying tractors and more land might increase their income, but it would certainly increase their indebtedness to the bank. Strengthening ties to the market meant weakening ties to their neighbors. The Country Life Movement emphasized individual farm success, not success through cooperative action with neighbors (Neth 1995, p. 191). Farmers in the more fertile lowlands closer to the village were in a better position to expand dairy production and to prosper. More isolated farmers were least able to afford investment in higher productivity, most committed to maintaining traditional exchange relationships with their neighbors, and most suspicious of tax raising initiatives to improve roads and schools. Farmers had modest expectations for rural life and mistrusted the advice of village outsiders.

The other goal of the Country Life Movement was to reduce the isolation and drudgery that made farm life unattractive by applying thinking in villages about current household design and management to the farm kitchen. Improving the roads connecting farm and village would also make rural life more satisfying. The automobile strengthened links between farm and village and quickly emerged as the farm's indispensable consumption item. By the late 1920s, 90 percent of farm families in New York owned a car (Barron 1997, p. 195). Young men and women learned how to drive and typically made several trips per week to the village. In the village, blacksmith shops were replaced by auto repair shops, wagon makers by auto dealerships and harness makers by gasoline stations. During hard times, farm families sacrificed running water, telephone and electricity before they gave up their automobile.

School consolidation was a priority of the Country Life Movement. Better roads would lower transportation costs to larger more distant schools, and economies of scale and specialization gains were available to larger consolidated schools. Larger schools could provide a more varied curriculum and better facilities. More specialized teachers could provide better teaching in math and science, art and foreign language. But local farmers were not convinced. Centralization required long wagon rides and exposure of children to saloons and moral looseness in village centers (Barron 1997, p. 60). Farmers objected to their loss of control over centralized schools which hired well qualified, modern teachers who trained their sons and daughters to be discontented with farm life, and raised their taxes in the process. Village merchants and craftsmen who sought to promote prosperity among rural farm customers were the principal champions of the Country Life Movement (Bowers, 1974, p. 30). School consolidation was the exception in rural New York until after World War II. In 1938, 250 central rural school districts peppered the New York State landscape amidst over 8000 one room school houses (Barron 1997, p. 74).

THE DECLINE OF DAIRY

The shift in cheese production from farm to factory after 1860 had brought conflict over the allocation of profits among dairy farmers and cheese manufacturers. The farmer typically received about 50 percent of each consumer dollar spent on cheese, the other 50 percent going to the cheese factory and to middlemen who transported the cheese to wholesale markets in New York City and England, promoted quality control, and smoothed out seasonal price fluctuations (Lampard 1963).

Dairy farmers were disadvantaged in their conflict with milk dealers over the distribution of the dollar among producers. New York City regulations to ensure the quality of milk sold within the city enabled milk dealers to set standards for milk accepted from individual dairy farmers. Farmers were required to purchase expensive milk pasteurizing equipment (Barron 1997, p. 89). Milk dealers had no incentive to interpret regulations loosely for the benefit of the dairy farmer, and as milk dealers became fewer and larger, they tended to pay farmers lower prices for raw milk.

Dillon (1941) asserts that dairy farmers received less than their fair share for the milk they produced. He argues that through sneaky practice and political connections, large dealers exercised monopoly power, paying milk producers low prices at the farm gate and overcharging urban consumers. Concentration of factories gave dairy processors an edge over the atomistic farm producers of raw milk in establishing prices. But Dillon overlooks the fact that large productivity gains were increasing supply and putting downward pressure on prices. Nationwide, milk production per cow increased by 40 percent between 1850 and 1910, primarily because better feeding and shelter allowed a longer milking season. Competition from efficient Middle Western producers, who produced feed at lower cost, was a larger factor in the decline of dairy in New York than price manipulations by a few large milk dealers.

From the 1880s and 1890s, rapid improvements in dairy productivity outstripped growth in demand, and dairy prices softened as a result. Prices recovered prior to World War I as dairy production stabilized and dairy products became an indispensable part of the urban diet. In the early twentieth century, progressive western New York farmers looked for ways to increase agricultural production for urban markets. They enlarged their farms by buying land from their neighbors. They specialized in dairy production, planting fewer food crops and converting their fields to pasture and corn. They increased productivity by reading agricultural journals and consulting with agricultural extension agents. Children and wives showed their accomplishments in raising better livestock and making a better home at annual agricultural fairs (Neth 1995, p. 97–121).

By the turn of the century, the long-term difficulties of dairy production in New York were already apparent, and by 1915, Wisconsin surpassed New York as the number one dairy producer. The key to dairy profitability was cheap feed, and western New York farmers could import feed from Midwestern states more cheaply than they could grow their own (Lampard 1963 p. 308).

Still, the Allegany County dairy industry flourished until about 1920. Demand for cheese rose faster than supply as workers in the growing industrial cities spent a portion of their rising incomes on dairy products. Also, canned condensed milk was included in the soldier's rations during World War I. The wholesale price of cheese in New York reached 29 cents per lb in 1920 but then fell sharply during the 1920s to 20 cents per lb in 1930 as Midwestern states increased milk production. Allegany County's population peaked at 43,200 in 1890, and then slipped to 41,400 in 1920 as smaller, less efficient farmers sold out to their larger neighbors and moved away.

When New York State dairy farmers confronted weak dairy prices, they discussed withholding production from the market in an effort to raise prices. Because farmers were so numerous, they had little success in coordinating their delivery of milk to the market in search of higher prices. A farmer might cheer on his neighbors to withhold milk production from the market in the hope of raising prices. But he might also figure that he would do best if he sells milk at the higher price won by his striking colleagues. This temptation to ride free on the efforts of others is a major obstacle to successful collective action (Olson 1965).

In this Prisoner's Dilemma, if a dairy farmer agreed with his neighbors to withhold their production from the market, all the farmers would be better off (3,3) as supply of milk would decline, demand would remain the same and milk prices paid to the producers would increase. But if a farmer double-crossed his neighbors by selling his milk to take advantage of the higher price, he would benefit at the expense of his neighbors. Market prices would decline, the strike would fail, and striking farmers would have succeeded only in enriching their greedy neighbors (4) at their own expense (1). Therefore, farmers would normally accept the low, unsatisfactory market price (2,2). They declined to take part in a strike action which might raise prices for all (3,3), because some neighbors would sell more than their fair share and gain a short term advantage (4,1) before prices fell again.

Formation of the Dairyman's League in 1916 was an example of an ultimately unsuccessful attempt to increase milk prices. At its peak, the League represented only 25 per cent of dairy cows in the eastern New York milk shed because many independent-minded farmers resented being told what to do by the Dairymen's League. Of those dairy farmers who did join the League, some cheated on their fellow strikers. A dairy farmer who shipped milk to dealers during the strike might not get caught, and if he were caught, he could bear the wrath of his neighbors (Barron 1997, p. 99).

During the Great Depression, farm prices collapsed as domestic demand for milk weakened and efficient farmers were able to increase production. The Agriculture Act of 1938 attempted to cut production, but individual farmers had every incentive to evade restrictions on their own production while hoping that the rules limited production of all other farmers (Cochrane and Ryan 1976, p. 23). In this Prisoner's Dilemma, all farmers are suffering from the collapse of prices caused in part by their efficient production (2,2). We will be better off if we all reduce production and prices rebound (3,3). But I will be better off if I can avoid reducing my output while everyone else is cutting theirs (4,1). All farmers want to avoid the worst outcome (1). When they refuse to cut their own production, they settle for (2) and are denied the benefits of higher prices (3).

Another unsuccessful dairy farmer effort to strengthen dairy prices was the Dairy Farmers Union (DFU) in 1936. The strength of the DFU was among small farmers in northern and central New York, and farmers in western New York did not join in large numbers. Farmers in northern and central New York were at the fringes of the New York City fluid milk shed, and prices for fluid milk fluctuated greatly. In western New York, milk went to cheese and butter production, where prices were more stable (Krieger 1997, p. 269). Also, well-established Allegany County farm families had less debt and were in better position to survive the hard times of the 1930s.

Tractors displaced the horse in the 1920s and converted agriculture into a capital intensive business. Many farmers mortgaged the farm to buy a tractor and to improve yields per acre by purchasing insecticides, fertilizers and better seed. The number of tractors on American farms increased from 147,000 in 1919 to 826,000 in 1929. Nationwide, agricultural output increased, and farm prices fell. For Midwestern farmers, dramatic increases in productivity compensated for declining milk prices (Flink 1988). But thin soils and a short growing season squeezed Allegany County farmers, whose productivity increases could not compensate for declining milk prices. By 1947, Allegany production of cheese had fallen by half from 1890 levels. The few remaining cheese factories were much larger and struggling to remain in business. In 1975, the single remaining factory produced 3.7 million pounds annually.

Table 6.1 shows that the national trend toward fewer, larger, more mechanized farms is apparent in Allegany County too. The number of farms

Table 6.1.   **Farming in Allegany County 1875–1998**

Year	N farms	Acres per farm	Total farm acres	N Dairy cows	Cows per dairy farm
1875	5920	106	NA	38,500	7
1945	3068	149	430,000	30,500	10
1998	150	192	164,000	11,500	77

Source: M.C. Bond, Allegany County: Agriculture and Land Use and New York Agricultural Statistics Service; Allegany County Farm Statistics, April 2000.

declined by 48 percent from 1875 to 1945. In the next 50 years, number of dairy farms plummeted to 150 by 1998. Today, only the stone foundations of many abandoned homesteads remain, and mature forest has reclaimed the former pastures.

The number of acres in farms declined 27 percent from 1875 to 1945 county wide, with every town declining. High elevation towns with thin soils and short growing seasons were the big losers. State forestation areas were distressed farms which New York State purchased at $4 per acre during the 1930s. Table 6.2 shows that the rate at which farms were abandoned from 1875–1945 varied from town to town. Land was settled much earlier in Alle-

The Greek Revival cornice detail indicates that this simple Elm Valley farmhouse was built around 1830, and the vegetation suggests that the farm was abandoned in the 1950s (author's photo).

Table 6.2. Percentage Decline, Land in Farms, 1875–1945

| | Allegany County Towns | |
Under 16% (8)	16%–38% (13)	over 38% (8)
Amity	Alfred	Alma
Caneadea	Almond	Birdsall
Friendship	Andover	Bolivar
Hume	Angelica	Genesee
Independence	Belfast	Ward
Rushford	Burns	West Almond
Wellsville	Centerville	Granger
Allen	Clarksville	Wirt
	Cuba	
	Grove	
	New Hudson	
	Scio	
	Willing	

Source: M. C. Bond, *Allegany County: Agriculture and Land Use*, Department of Agricultural Economics, Cornell University, Ithaca NY, 1947.

gany towns where transportation was more convenient and growing conditions better, and in these towns dairy farming survived well into the twentieth century.

In low lying valley towns where the soil was richer and mean temperature slightly higher (Amity, Caneadea, Friendship), the decline in farming acreage from 1875 to 1945 was less than 16 percent. These were the towns in which the first settlers chose to settle 200 years ago. Years were required to build a successful dairy farm; the Census of 1855 reveals that heads of household producing cheese were older (47 years) than the average head of household (41 years) and had been working their land for much longer (22 years) than the average head of household (14years).

In the high elevation towns (Birdsall, Bolivar, Granger), farm acreage declined by over one-third from 1875 to 1945. Early settlers tended to avoid those towns that were distant from transportation routes and where soils were thin.[1] For the 29 towns of Allegany County, farmers in the towns that were settled later took longer to clear the land and begin dairy production. When the depression hit in 1929, the already hard pressed dairy farmers on Turnpike Road and in all of the upland areas that are now state forest land saw the handwriting on the wall. They were the first to abandon dairy production after the 1920s.

To illustrate, compare the fate of farms at different locations in the town of Almond. Farms along Turnpike Road have thin soils and are located at high elevation. Low-lying Karr Valley farms have good soils. Initially, Turnpike

Road farmers shared in the prosperity brought by completion of the railroad and expansion of the dairy industry. A large 250 acre parcel that sold for $10 in 1867 doubled in value 15 years later in 1882. And I. N. Helmer built a cheese factory as late as 1892, using the milk of 100 Turnpike Road cows.

When dairy prices collapsed during the Great Depression, Allegany County farmers could not sell milk and cover their costs of production. All of the land along Turnpike Road was sold to New York State at $4 per acre during the 1930s. Sellers also retained the right to cut marketable timber (over 12 inches in diameter), to pasture animals and to remove buildings and fences for a period of one year after sale. A survey of 26 property deeds recorded in the Allegany County Court House, Belmont, indicates that about half of the sellers lived in various cities outside the Almond area, and many of the remaining sellers lived in Almond, Arkport, Hornell and other local villages. These descendants of the original Turnpike Road farmers had largely abandoned their lands and had no better offer than New York State's $4 per acre. Often adult children had moved away from their Turnpike Road homes and sold to the state upon the death of their parents. Today Turnpike Road is uninhabited and lined with mature stands of mixed second growth forest and plantation stands of red pine.

The story in Karr Valley during the Great Depression unfolded quite differently. Only less desirable land away from the road was sold to New York

Local farmers used Pine Hill behind Alfred University to the south west to feed their dairy cattle in 1900. Alumni Hall is in the center of the photograph (Herrick Library, Alfred University).

Today, dairy farming is in demise, and Pine Hill is completely reforested. Alumni Hall is in the center of the photograph behind the tall smoke stack (author's photo).

State. Most Karr Valley farmers held on to their land during the Great Depression even as they cut back on agricultural production. One holding that had changed hands for $49 per acre in 1918 sold for $34 per acre in 1934 (Index of Deeds, Allegany County, Belmont NY). Valley lands were transferred to young relatives willing to continue living on the land.

Lands that were pasture in 1900 were abandoned by 1950 and have reverted to mature forest, as these Pine Hill photographs show.

The pastures on Pine Hill behind Alfred University in 1900 have been reforested today.

THE POLITICS OF AGRICULTURAL DECLINE

In 1900, most political issues affecting daily lives were resolved at the local level. Local elected officials worked hard to avoid political conflict within the community, seeking to build consensus or to reach a compromise with broad support before raising contentious issues on school funding and road construction and maintenance (Baker 1991). Local elected officials preferred to build solidarity by enacting policies broadly acceptable within the community, and sought to avoid sharp, zero-sum conflict between advocates of holding taxes down and improving public services. Town political differences always reflected local and factional politics. In high elevation, more distant towns in decline, advocates of low taxes and limited government services tended to dominate political discussion. In growing towns, progressive farmers and civic boosters were strong advocates of better schools and improved roads (Baker 1991, p. 93). One way to avoid conflict was to ask New York

State for the funds needed to improve roads and schools. Local voters complained that state funding meant loss of local autonomy, but as rural areas were overrepresented in Albany, the distribution of state funds worked in their favor.

Participation in politics was an exclusively male privilege until extension of the franchise to women in 1917. Church-related women's clubs in Alfred and Cuba actively supported women's suffrage, but many women viewed political activity as the proper domain of men. In the nineteenth century, politics had been very much the province of men, and women exercised their influence within the home. Women were isolated from the grubby business of politics and commerce, which underlined their moral superiority. By the end of the century, women were articulating their interests in local politics. Rural men wished to limit local government activity to keep taxes low; women called upon government to restrict the sale of alcohol. The votes of men extended the vote to women, and the perception in the following decades was that women did not vote differently than did their husbands and fathers (Baker 1991, p. 30).

Nationally, political party conflict centered on the relative prosperity of agricultural and industrial interests. The center of Republican political

These Fillmore area women marched in support of women's suffrage in 1917 (Allegany County Historian).

party dominance in the north shifted from the rural county courthouse to the growing industrial and commercial cities. In rural areas of the west and south, the most powerful issue in 1896 had been the decline in the price of agricultural commodities, like grain and cotton, relative to the price of industrial manufactures. Farmers in the South and the Plains states supported Populist Democrat William Jennings Bryan to protest low agricultural prices. But for several reasons, Bryan had little support in western New York and Republican Party dominance continued without interruption. Dairy production was less susceptible than cotton, wheat and corn to weather related boom and bust cycles in prices (Sundquist 1983, p. 139). Urban demand for dairy products was steady. Northern farmers could resort to subsistence-oriented mixed farming during hard times, given better soil and rainfall conditions. Third generation farmers in western New York had inherited their farms and were not saddled with debt. Kinship ties between farmers and village residents eased tensions between countryside and town (Barron 1984). And discontented western New Yorkers had the option of migrating to prosperous cities nearby. Allegany County gave Populists over eight percent of the vote in the 1890s, their best showing in New York State. Economically hard pressed towns like Ward led the way.

The Democratic Party's program of higher prices for agricultural commodities might have appealed to western New York farmers, but they remained sympathetic to Protestant moral values of prohibition and restriction of European immigration championed by Republicans (Sundquist 1983, p. 168). As economic conditions worsened again after World War I, western New York rural voters remained loyally Republican. Despite the hardships of the Great Depression, Franklin Delano Roosevelt's New Deal shifted few votes from Republican to Democrat in western New York. In rural New York counties, Democrats won about 30 percent of the vote in the 1920s, soared to about 45 per cent in the depression year of 1932, and then gradually declined to a steady 35 percent in the 1940s (Sundquist 1983, p. 216).

Upstate voters remained loyally Republican because they suspected that downstate interests dominated state government. Also, in the depression year of 1928 when the Democratic Party nominated Catholic Al Smith as their candidate for president, the issues of prohibition and Catholicism continued to hold rural Republican voters, who ignored Democratic Party promises to stabilize farm prices. The urban poor, trade unions and urban political machines were the core of Roosevelt's political strength (Jensen 1981, p. 210).

IMPACT OF THE AUTOMOBILE

Development of a gear system and the light weight pneumatic tire popularized the bicycle in the 1870s and 1880s. With a bicycle, a family member could travel to town quickly and at a time of one's choosing. Bicycle riders demanded road improvements, a pressing local political issue (Baker 1991). The first generation of automobile owners, prosperous villagers who drove their cars out into the bucolic countryside, also wanted road improvements. Many rural localities passed laws to address problems of trespass, animals frightened by fast traveling, noisy automobiles, and rude behavior by the owners of the "devil wagons" (Berger 1979, p. 26).

The automobile, particularly Henry Ford's Model T, quickly transformed personal transport in rural America. It appeared to Ford that "everyone wants to be somewhere he isn't. As soon as he gets there, he wants to go right back" (Constable n.d.). In 1908, 6000 Model Ts were sold; by 1916 Ford sold 577,000 cars, claimed one half of the U.S. auto market and dominated sales to western New York farmers. The Model T was durable, easy to operate and repair, and affordable. The price dropped from $850 in 1908 to $360 in 1916, and a pleased Henry Ford observed "Every time I lower the price a dollar, we gain a thousand new buyers" (Constable n.d.).

Wood frame commercial buildings in Centerville around 1915. Farm families still rely on horse and buggy, but a shop owner has an automobile and bicycles provide individual transportation. Above the store is an apartment. The street is not yet paved, but electricity is now available in the village (Hinkle Library, Alfred State College).

Increasingly heavy traffic visiting shops in Cuba led the village to pave Main Street. Paving was a labor intensive process. The bricks are stacked on the sidewalk in the center of the photograph. This paving project precedes the automobile, which spread rapidly after 1910. With the automobile, Western New York farm families could more easily reach larger commercial centers like Cuba and Wellsville (Allegany County Historian).

Even as dairy prices fell in the 1920s, the hard-pressed farmer's purchase of a \$300 Model T was a family priority (Berger 1979, p. 44). The first car appeared in the village of Fillmore in 1906, and some 200 Fillmore residents enjoyed their first automobile ride in that car. By 1912, residents of Fillmore owned 25 automobiles. As early as 1922, 864 cars passed through downtown Fillmore's main intersection on a Saturday, and in the mid-1920s, most Allegany County farmers owned a Model T Ford (Smith 1995).

Many women learned to drive in the 1920s and could dash into town in the middle of a busy day. Usually their destination was the closest village, but increasingly they traveled to department store or supermarket in a more distant regional village like Wellsville, Warsaw or Hornell. They could visit the specialized shops on Main Street, where a greater variety of larger shops offered more varied goods at lower prices. Farmers could obtain necessary supplies at the hardware store or Agway.

The automobile quickly became indispensable to the social life of the farm family. Older and younger women unburdened by child care responsibilities could go to the village and return in a few hours. Women in cars tended to visit the village rather than their neighbors. In town they could attend meetings at church, visit with friends, learn the latest ideas in home management, and see the latest implements found in the typical modern home (Baker 1991, p. 58). The automobile became the single indispensable appliance; as one woman reported, "you can't go to town in a bathtub" (Scharff 1991, p. 144). As women began to work in larger numbers and the automobile carried farm women to village activities, the family that had provided most social guidance, control and services for family members began to loosen its hold (Ryan 1981, p. 241).

In rural villages, automobile sales lagged among those residents who easily walked to the village center on a daily basis to buy food, clothing and hardware. On the way, they chatted with neighbors sitting on their front porches and exchanged greetings at the post office. Urban streetcars also transported residents between a few neighboring villages.

The automobile also encouraged construction of housing further from the commercial center, in both cities and rural villages of western New York. In the cities many residents continued to walk to neighborhood stores or factories, and to travel longer distances on the street car or train. Urbanites who desired to move into the new suburban areas that extended outward along new roads and streetcar paths purchased automobiles. Automobile ownership and suburban sprawl are the signature characteristics of urban America in the twentieth century. In every decade since 1900, the suburban population of

The street car between Olean and Wellsville provided regular transportation for residents of Little Genesee around the turn of the century (Bolivar Library).

cities like Rochester and Buffalo has grown faster than the central city population (Judd 2002).

By 1940, Allegany County women were escaping the rigors of farm life at a slightly faster rate than men. Most females in 1940 still worked at home and were not counted in the labor force. Males in the work force outnumbered females by four to one. Women were more likely than men to move from farm to village. In 1940, 2400 females found jobs in wholesale and retail trade, domestic services and traditionally female professional occupations like teaching and nursing. Allegany County's population was 50.5 percent male in 1940, but the average number of males recorded in the villages of Andover, Belmont, Bolivar, Cuba and Friendship was 47.8 percent (US Census, 1940.)[2]

HOUSING STYLES IN THE AUTOMOBILE AGE

Our homes express important ideas about family and community. Porches, for example, are a standing invitation to neighbors and multiple special purpose rooms invite privacy within the family. Homes reflect our changing economic fortunes; as we have become more prosperous, our homes have generally grown larger and incorporated the latest in architectural fashion. In the age of the automobile, women sought ways to simplify the complex tasks of keeping a home. In the 1920s, the decorative excess of Queen Anne Victorian homes gave way to the clean lines and utilitarian convenience of the bungalow.

Architects and builders introduced the bungalow in California, and from the West Coast the idea spread eastward after 1915. Most Allegany County villages have examples of bungalows that were built in the 1920s. The long roof covers both porch and house, emphasizing the unity of indoor and outdoor environment. Bungalow builders valued natural materials—wood, fieldstone and tile. Large dormers were cut into the roofline to add well-lighted bedroom space. The irregular, over-scaled porch piers suggest natural complexity rather than the rational symmetry of the Greek Revival era.

Many ideas incorporated into the bungalow reflect contemporary ideas of how women could accomplish their role as household manager expeditiously. While women in the 1920s lived more of their lives outside the home, their primary responsibility was to manage the household and raise the children. Bungalow designers tried to make the job easier. Bedrooms, bathroom and kitchen were small but organized efficiently. Bookshelves and ironing boards were built into the walls. The mirror in the bathroom doubled as the door of the hidden medicine cabinet. One large room served as parlor, dining area and family room, replacing the multiple single purpose rooms of the Victorian

Sears Roebuck and other companies sold complete housing kits at affordable prices. The components for this bungalow in the village of Fillmore were cut and crated in a factory, shipped by rail to the site, and assembled there (author's photo).

This Wellsville bungalow features a large upstairs dormer and a porte cochere to protect the family from the elements as they entered the house from carriage or automobile (author's photo).

era. Furniture and home decoration favored arts and crafts simplicity. Builders and designers favored clean lines and practicality. Dust catching Victorian bric-a-brac cluttering every surface fell out of fashion (Wright 1980).

In the early twentieth century, progressive reformers advocated housing that ordinary workers could afford. For the first time, banks offered low cost mortgage loans that enabled potential homeowners to build now and pay later. Indoor plumbing and electrification increased costs, but higher costs were partially offset by standardized plans and factory precut materials. Home ownership came within the reach of many working class Americans. Incomes rose faster than construction costs. The construction industry advertised extensively to make young families aware that buying their own home was within reach.

John Jakle (1989) has counted and dated the housing stock in several communities over a 200-year period. His information on the age of dwellings in Cazenovia, New York, suggests that about 16 percent of the housing stock in

This cross gable working class cottage with two and a half stories and a basement was built in the village of Almond in 1907. The upstairs attic served as a sleeping area for extra children or boarders. In cities, this cottage evolved into the two story duplex consisting of upper and lower flats or two side by side units sharing a common wall. Notice the lovely gable end window decorations. You can find these cottages on "Main Street" away from the village center or on village side streets. In the oldest portion of town adjacent to the central business district, older Greek Revival, Italianate and Victorian Queen Anne and shingle styles are likely to dominate (author's photo).

Allegany County was probably built before 1865. Why only 16 percent when the population of Allegany County held steady for the century from 1865 to 1970? First, fewer houses accommodated the Allegany County population in 1865. The 1855 census reports 5.2 persons per household, compared to 3.2 persons in 1965. An 1865 home typically housed a nuclear family plus an aging parent, a young dependent relative or perhaps a servant or hired hand. Second, many pre-1965 homes have not survived the rigors of time. Some poorly constructed or unfashionable homes were torn down, or washed away in floods. In an age when flames burned continuously to heat and light interiors, fire was a frequent, dreaded visitor to homes and businesses typically constructed entirely of wooden materials above the foundation. Long time residents of Rushford village estimated in 1908 that 68 homes had been destroyed in the village (Merrill 1908).

Because of the specter of fire, residents of all towns donated time, energy, and cash to purchase up-to-date fire fighting equipment and to build a fire hall to accommodate the equipment. Fire insurance became available in the 1890s, and towns with modern fire fighting apparatus and an adequate water supply enjoyed lower insurance rates. A major fire in Canaseraga village in 1900 destroyed over 100 buildings in the village center, the flames fanned by strong winds. Homes and businesses were rebuilt quickly; within 10 years store owners erected the brick buildings that define the Canaseraga village center today. As in Canaseraga, merchants in virtually all western New York villages rebuilt their business districts out of brick early in the twentieth century to resist fire—and to reflect their confidence in the future.

These local fire fighters do their best to extinguish flames and prevent the fire from spreading (Allegany County Historian)

Few houses were built in western New York between 1920 and 1945 (Jakle et. al., 1989). Falling dairy prices pressured western new York dairy farmers in the 1920s and 1930s, dealing a heavy blow to local village economies. In the early 1940s, little housing was built as the war effort consumed all material resources and labor power. Probably over a third of Allegany county's housing has been constructed since 1945, and this housing stock is predominantly ranch homes and manufactured housing.

Historic changes in transportation costs and economies of scale that served western New York well before 1920 began to work against the region, especially after World War II. Rapid improvements in automobile and highways rendered the railroad obsolete. With the automobile, people could travel greater distances quickly. Local villages withered as people drove to large regional villages 12 miles away or to regional cities 50 miles distant. In these commercial centers, merchants offered a wider variety of specialized goods and services at low cost and employers offered higher wage jobs. Individual dairy farms and local village economies have been hit hard. What will the future bring to western New York and Allegany County?

NOTES

1. Statistically, the simple correlation between estimated town population in 1830 and the decline in farm acreage from 1875 to 1945 is .409, significant at the .05 level.

2. Gender differences between county and village populations are statistically significant: $X2 = 10.135, p = .0013, DF = 1$.

Chapter Seven

Life in a Barely Agricultural Western New York: 1950–Present

Since World War II, Allegany County's core dairy industry has continued to decline. This decline has affected who lives in Allegany County, their standard of living, the houses they live in, and their natural environment. Changing transportation costs as truck and automobile replaced the railroad after World War II help to explain these social changes. Also, specialization and economies of scale have hurt the competitive position of local dairy farms, local manufacturing plants and retail stores. Small villages like Friendship and Fillmore are no longer the commercial centers they were before World War II.

CHANGES IN THE RURAL ECONOMY

Former dairy pastures have reverted to forest, raising interesting questions about the quality of life in an increasingly forested environment and possible new land uses, such as tourism or waste disposal. As transportation costs for local residents have declined with the automobile, people have built their homes on low-cost abandoned farm land outside the villages. Western New York faces many economic challenges, but some opportunities promise a viable future.

Over the last 50 years, the Allegany County economy has become less dependent on agriculture and, to a lesser extent, manufacturing. Table 7.1 illustrates structural changes in the Allegany County economy over the last 50 years.

By 1980, farming provided only 5.5 percent of the employment in Allegany County, down from 26 percent in 1940. Many women worked for wages

Table 7.1. Allegany County: Employees by Industry, 1950 and 2000

| | 1950 | | 2000 | |
Sector	N	%	N	%
Manufacturing	3544	23.7%	3588	16.7%
Agriculture, Mining, Forestry	3875	25.9%	813	3.8%
Wholesale and Retail Trade	1739	11.6%	2686	12.5%
Accommodation and Food	661	4.4%	1597	7.4%
Education	1323	8.8%	5032	23.3%
Health and Social Assistance	289	1.9%	1939	9.0%
State and Local Government	425	2.8%	777	3.6%
Construction	791	5.3%	1356	6.3%
Other	2296	15.4%	3767	17.4%
Total	14944	99.8%	21555	100.0%

Source: US Census Data, 1950 and 2000

in 1980, 42 percent of the labor force being female. Allegany County women today whose grandmothers and great grandmothers worked on the farm now are wage earners in factories, schools and retail sales. Workforce participation gives females more equal status within the household and a better opportunity to escape from an unsatisfactory marriage, as historically high divorce rates indicate. Contemporary two-income families once again resemble a common household enterprise more than the separate spheres where the male worked in field and factory to provide income and the female maintained the home and nurtured the children.

The rural Allegany County economy is shaped differently from the more urban state economy, as shown in the earnings by sector in Table 7.2. The manufacturing sector in a rural county is smaller than the state average because factories are located far from raw materials and their urban customers, and transportation costs are high. Most manufacturing establishments are small, having fewer than 100 employees on the payroll. Two large manufacturers, Wellsville-based Alstom Preheater and Dresser Rand, have employed

Table 7.2. Earnings by Sector, Allegany County and New York State 2000

Sector	Allegany County	New York State
Manufacturing, Mining, Construction	6.4%	15.3%
Retail Trade	9.5%	6.4%
Finance, insurance, real estate	21.8%	20.7%
Services	24.3%	31.0%
Government	26.7%	14.5%
Other	1.2%	12.0%

Source: U S Census Bureau, County and City Data Book: 2000, Tables B5, B7, B8, B13

over 500 workers. Villages that are the centers of manufacturing activity and services, Wellsville, Alfred, and Cuba, have seen modest population growth since 1940.

Economic expansion is concentrated in the service sector. Working women spend less time in the kitchen and more time at the mall, as the expansion of retail trade and restaurant service indicates. Retail trade is strong because consumers prefer not to drive long distances to purchase items like groceries, automobile repairs, insurance and banking, routine medical services and restaurant meals that are available locally. The reality of transportation costs guarantees that local residents will continue to support local businesses. Retail trade is also strong because low-income Allegany County residents spend more than they earn, thanks to governmental income redistribution policies.

Many services in Allegany County are provided by local school districts, county agencies, and higher education and other government service providers. Both Alfred University and Alfred State College of Technology more than doubled their student populations from 1950 to 2000, and these institutions are now the largest employers in the county.

The demise of the railroad after World War II hurt the local economy, as did construction of the interstate highway system that bypassed Allegany

In the 1930s, Wellsville was a major commercial center in the Southern Tier, attracting people from about a 15 mile radius. They regularly purchased goods and services in dozens of successful shops along Main Street (Allegany County Historian).

Burrous Furniture store served the Wellsville area until the owners closed its doors in the 1990s. Area residents now routinely travel to Rochester or Buffalo for their furniture needs (author's photo).

Newberry's department store closed its doors in the 1990s. Today the building houses physical therapy center, catering to an aging population, and a marine recruiting office, underlining the lack of job opportunities for young people in the area (author's photo).

County. East/west traffic tended to follow Interstate 90 through northern New York or Interstate 80 through central Pennsylvania. Downtown Wellsville, which had been a bustling commercial center for decades before World War II, went into decline. Suburban shopping malls with ample parking and larger stores hurt downtown Wellsville businesses. Local consumers drove to Rochester and Buffalo to spend more of their dollars.

FUTURE OF THE WESTERN NEW YORK DAIRY FARM

Many rural communities primarily based on agriculture are now settings for deepening poverty and lack of opportunity, compared to contemporary urban communities (Fitchen 1991; Lyson and Falk, 1993). Post World War II agricultural policies have promoted dramatic increases in productivity. Successful farms required new fertilizers, seeds, milking machines and harvesting equipment, and few Allegany County dairy farms have been unable to compete with large, well capitalized Midwestern dairy farms. As agricultural productivity has increased, demand for agricultural products has grown more slowly. In an effort to balance supply and demand, the federal government has donated surplus grain and dairy products to school nutrition programs, promoted food stamp programs, and exported food to distressed areas overseas. But supply increases have consistently outpaced demand growth. The winners have been large well-capitalized farmers, and the needs of low-production farm families and non farm families living in poverty have largely gone unaddressed (Cochrane and Ryan 1976, p. 115; Friedberger 1988, p. 11).

Only 3.4 percent of the Allegany County population earned a share of their income from farm production in 1990. And farm income constitutes only one percent of Allegany County income. The average value of farm products sold is about $48,000 per farm, which is probably typical for the 77 percent of intermediate size Allegany County farms. Most farms in Allegany County are neither very small (14 percent are less than 50 acres) or very large (9 percent are over 500 acres).

After one subtracts out-of-pocket costs of producing and marketing milk, beef, Christmas trees or maple syrup, hardly enough is left to pay the farm operator a living wage. Very often, the farm is supported by the earnings from one or more adult workers who earn an income working in retail sales or teaching school in a neighboring community. Agriculture is much more attractive in Allegany's neighboring counties to the north where soils are better and the growing season longer. Genesee County farms yield an average of $212,000 in annual sales, and Livingston County farms gross $117,000 in annual sales.

Today about 150 dairy farms remain in Allegany County and they generate 74 percent of the value of agricultural products (Allegany County Farm Statistics 2000). Remaining dairy farms in 2000 are widely distributed, concentrated in towns that were settled early and abandoned late. Most of these dairy farms are concentrated in 12 towns located along major roads, not because transportation costs are lower but because major roads run through more fertile, low level valleys with higher mean temperatures. The Allegany River basin towns—Clarksville, Genesee, Bolivar and Alma—are under represented with a total of three farms. The Northwest towns—Centerville, Hume, Rushford and Caneadea—are over represented, averaging 11 farms per town. Opportunities for sharing labor, knowledge, equipment and social support could explain this concentration.

Even at the peak of dairy prosperity in the late nineteenth century, the dairy industry in Allegany County and in New York State began to decline. The decline in dairy accelerated during the Great Depression of the 1930s, when urban workers lost their jobs, demand for dairy products fell and producer prices collapsed (Bond 1947). Most of the state forestland was purchased by New York State from bankrupt farmers in the 1930s.

In the late 1970s, rapidly rising energy prices fueled an inflationary price surge and high levels of unemployment which cut into demand for dairy products. Even worse, dairy farmers typically borrowed money to buy land and machinery, and interest rates reaching double digit levels in the 1980s imposed a crushing debt burden on the hard pressed dairy farmer. Agway, which had thrived as a supplier of farm needs, attempted to survive as a lawn and garden store but closed its doors in the mid 1990s.

Today, fewer but larger farms are producing more milk than ever. The average size of Allegany County farms increased from 106 acres in 1875 to 149 acres in 1945 to 192 acres in 1998. Allegany County ranks thirteenth in the state for number of farms and twentieth for amount of land in farms, indicating that Allegany farms tend to be smaller than the state average (New York Agricultural Statistics Service, 2000). About a dozen large dairy farms milk over 200 head of cattle. Several dozen small farmers make a living milking about 15 cattle. In 1997, average net income from farming operations was about $8700. Some farmers find high value market niches such as organic milk production and a few Amish farmers survive by hand-milking small herds. Many farmers rely upon off-farm income; only 48 percent of Allegany farm operators report that farming is their principal occupation. Some farmers simply make do with very modest incomes. Dairy production continues because land is inexpensive; the farmer can compensate for low per acre yields by using more acres for pasturing cows and growing feed.

Nationwide, demand for dairy products is not keeping pace with supply, and the price that dairy farmers receive for their product does not keep pace with their rising costs. Wisconsin's share of cheese production is down to 27 percent, and New York now produces only nine percent of the nation's cheese. In both states, the small family farm, milking about 80 head, dominates production. This tradition faces a strong challenge from California and other western states where industrial agriculture prevails. These agribusiness operations typically milk 650–1000 head, and yields per cow are higher on these large farms. In California today, yields are 21,000 pounds of milk per year compared to 17,000 in Wisconsin (Barboza 2001). Small family farms cannot match their lower capital and labor costs per gallon.

To increase the profitability of dairy farming, milk producers today seek to raise the price of milk through subsidies paid by consumers and taxpayers. The Northeast Interstate Dairy Compact guarantees farmers in the six New England states a minimum price per gallon for the milk they market. New York is seeking to join the compact so its dairy farmers can have access to this price subsidy. Opponents to expanding the government price support program are the dairy rich Midwestern states, who are low cost producers; urban consumers, who object to poor families with children paying an extra 15 cents per gallon to subsidize milk producers; and free traders who argue that low prices will stimulate dairy export markets around the world (Tierney 1999).

In 1960, farming was exclusively a male occupation. Twelve percent of the county's male labor force was engaged in farming, less than one percent of females (32 individuals) were counted as farmers. By 1980, men still farming declined to eight percent, while women engaged in farming increased five-fold to 2.1 percent of the work force. Apparently in some small family dairy operations, men found employment off the farm, while their female partners tended to daily farm chores. Amish farmers, forced to sell their farms in Pennsylvania because of high taxes, have been attracted to Allegany County by low per acre land costs.

Today's farmers are generally descendants of farmers. The key to maintaining the small family dairy farm is the willingness of a son or daughter to take over the family business. This factor is critical in the next decade, as the current average age of farm operators is 53 years (Allegany County Farm Statistics 2000). Most children of dairy farmers have pursued more lucrative off-farm economic opportunities. The few who choose to continue the family dairy farm come from towns located throughout the county. Their commitment outweighs marginal variations in land quality that led earlier generations of farmers to prefer some towns, and to abandon farms earlier in less desirable towns.

The long-term decline of the small family farm in western New York is likely to continue. Larger scale operations benefit from economies of scale and higher productivity. Any price subsidies won under the dairy compacts will not erase that competitive disadvantage. The struggle to preserve the family farm continues against considerable odds. A rural landscape painted with grazing black and white Holsteins, a white Greek revival farmhouse and a red barn with corn-filled silos charms the viewer. From 1850–1950, Allegany was a county of middling prosperity by the standards of the day. Today, because of post World War II transportation decisions, the economic decline of New York State, and the concentration of economic activity in city and suburb, Allegany County now ranks 60 out of 62 New York State counties in per capita income. The family dairy farm, while no longer a large contributor to the county economy, has a mythic importance as a reminder of an earlier period of economic prosperity. The children of aging dairy farmers have grown up in a post World War II, consumption-oriented material culture. They have options to pursue more lucrative off-farm career opportunities. How many will continue to choose dairy farming as a way of life in the coming decade?

POPULATION TRENDS IN ALLEGANY COUNTY

Allegany County's population count has increased since 1950 after a century of stability. In 1840, after three decades of rapid population growth based on immigration and land clearing, Allegany County counted a population of about 40,000. Population then remained nearly constant for the next one hundred years, even as population in the cities and suburbs of New York grew rapidly. After 1950, population slowly increased, peaking at 51,472 in 1980. After 1980, population declined to 50,470 (-2.5 percent) in 1990 and to 49,927 (-1.1 percent) in 2000, while New York State as a whole gained over a million residents. Still, Allegany County's population has increased by 20 percent between 1950 and 2000, even though Allegany County was the second poorest county in New York State, measured by per capita income.

The age distribution of the Allegany County population, compared to New York State as a whole, favors the very young and the very old; age groups that are not part of the labor force (Lowry 1966).

Because Allegany County is home to three colleges, the population in the 18–24 brackets is well above the state average. But because young people in Allegany County cannot easily find work locally and move elsewhere in search of opportunity, the 25–44 age group is small, as is the under age five

Table 7.3.   Population by Age Group

	Population by Age Group In 2000 (percent)					Social Security per 100 Recipients
	Under 5	5–17	18–24	25–44	45–64	over 65
New York State	6.5%	18.2%	9.3%	30.7%	22.3%	12.8%	163
Allegany County	5.6%	18.8%	15.5%	23.9%	22.2%	14.1%	188

Source: US Census Bureau, County and City Data Book 2000

grouping. Finally, Allegany County has a large population over age 65 compared to the New York State average.

Since the 25–44 age group is so small, why has population increased since 1950? One reason is an artifact of census taking procedures. In 1980, the Census Bureau began to count college students as residing at their college address, not as residing in their parents' home. This change followed extension of the right to vote to 18-year-olds in 1971 as part of a trend to treat young people as responsible adults, rather than as children dependent upon their parents. About half of the increase in 1980 is in the towns of Alfred and Caneadea, where Alfred State College of Technology, Alfred University and Houghton College are located.

Some people are able to live in Allegany County because transfer payments from state and federal governments help to support the contemporary service economy. Allegany County's large population over age 65 spends their social security checks and Medicare payments at local grocery stores and health care clinics (Table 7.3). Some taxes paid to the state are returned to the localities to support K-12 education and county public works and social service programs. Under the New York State tax system, wealthy suburban counties tend to pay more than they receive from the state, while poor counties like Allegany receive more funds from the state than they pay in taxes to hire teachers and purchase capital equipment. Three quarters of Medicaid costs for eligible low income residents are paid at the state and federal level. New York State returns 39 percent of its budget to local governments, ranking sixth among the American states.

Finally, many Allegany County residents prefer to live near family and friends and treasure familiar places and routines. Why move to a distant unknown place that inevitably involves risk and uncertainty? (Richardson 1973). For many, the beautiful forested hills, clean air and sense of neighborliness and community compare favorably to the congestion, crime, and pollution of more heavily populated counties. Children can more easily participate in their favorite activities at a smaller school, and their parents can more easily be involved in community affairs.

Allegany County workers have an easy commute. The average travel time to work is 17 minutes for the Allegany County worker, compared to a state average of 32 minutes (US Statistical Abstract 2005, p. 694). A few people do commute long distances to work every day, and they regret the tedium of the journey and the out of pocket cost to maintain the car and fill the gas tank. But compensating advantages are not difficult to find. As the county has lost population relative to other New York counties, land and housing prices have fallen. Now Allegany County appeals to buyers who want 20 acres of land to keep horses, hunt or hike, and be close to nature. A house that costs $80,000 in Belfast or Friendship might cost $200,000 in suburban Rochester or Buffalo. For some local residents, the lower price offsets the cost of commuting 50 miles to work.

MEASURING ECONOMIC AND SOCIAL WELL BEING

Allegany County and the other rural counties of western New York lag well behind New York State on various measures of income, unemployment and health care (Table 7.4).

Small villages have been particularly hard hit. Many small businesses that once flourished, like the Friendship Hotel, have closed their doors. Many local villages withered on the vine, as residents drove quickly to a large regional village fifteen miles distant or to a city 60 miles away. There, consumers shopped at supermarkets and large retail stores that offered greater choices at lower prices than could local, small volume retailers.

Many small factories that produced roofing tiles, textiles and canned goods could no longer compete. They were closed down, their production being shifted to more efficient factories closer to consumers in suburban communities, or relocated in the American South, or to low wage factories in Mexico or China. Local service oriented economies in 2006 bear little resemblance to the dairy based economy of a century ago.

Table 7.4.   Measures of Economic Well Being: Allegany County New York State

Indicator	Allegany County	New York State
Per Capita Income	$17,444	$32,108
Median Household Income	$31,291	$36,369
Unemployment Rate	6.7%	4.6%
Persons below Poverty Line	18.1%	15.6%
Physicians Per Capita	91 per 100,000	395 per 100,000
Hospital Beds	138 per 100,000	377 per 100,000

Source: U S Census Bureau, County and City Data Book 2000

The New Friendship Hotel welcomed many commercial visitors to Friendship in 1911 (Allegany County Historian).

In 2006, the abandoned Friendship hotel has suffered extensive water damage and will likely be torn down. The white clapboard building across the street is also vacant. Few passers-by have business in Friendship, and they are likely to stay in a motel along Route 86. Friendship residents shop in Wellsville or Buffalo (author's photo).

THE AUTOMOBILE AND HOUSING PATTERNS

With the end of World War II, returning GIs married their girl friends, started families and used their savings and GI loans to build homes. About a third of western New York housing was built after 1945 (Jakle 1989). The automobile shaped the style and location of this new housing stock. For several decades, the ranch style home dominated the post World War II housing vocabulary. Ranch homes, modeled on nineteenth century western buildings, originated in California in the 1930s. Ranches were single story with a gently sloping roof that gives the home a horizontal look. Ranch homes popularized some of the ideas worked out in the prairie style of Frank Lloyd Wright, who struggled against the classical vocabulary of balance and proportion, of columns and cornices. Wright also rejected the Victorian practice of dividing interiors into a series of boxlike special purpose rooms. Dividing space into a reception hall, library, sewing room and bedroom quite literally built walls between family members. Wright organized his interiors as a single flowing space, and ranch houses continued this practice (Moore 2002).

The post World War II housing boom centered on construction of homes on the village outskirts and beyond. Property was less costly outside of the village as farming declined, so home buyers could afford larger lots beyond the village center. Many suburban style neighborhoods sprang up several blocks distant from the village center since people could drive the six blocks to shop in the village center. Along county and state highways, land costs and taxes were lower than in villages. The automobile enabled people to locate their homes on these rural roads and not be isolated from friends and family. High land values in more densely populated villages favor construction of three or more story apartments, which are common in urban centers and suburban communities. But almost no apartment complexes are being built today in Allegany County; in the year 2000, 100 percent of the building permits issued were for single unit housing, compared to half of the building permits statewide.

The long axis of a rectangular shaped ranch is parallel to the street to convey a sense of size. Bedrooms are at one end of the house and the kitchen and living areas occupy a large open space at the other end. The kitchen served as a convenient command post where the woman kept track of younger children's activities while preparing the family's dinner.

Most families now owned an automobile, and the garage was often added to the house, accentuating the long low horizontal look. The family typically entered the house into the kitchen, the entrance being conveniently located near the garage. The automobile also transformed the front door and the porch area of the family home. Family members and even visitors entered the house

The automobile enabled home builders to afford low cost, larger lots on the outskirts of town and to build sprawling ranch style homes. The garage is an integral part of this Belmont area home, and the front door serves mostly as an emergency exit (author's photo).

through the kitchen. The front door, which had been the gateway into the home for the visitor in both classical and Victorian times, lost its purpose.

With passersby now driving past the house in cars at 30 miles per hour, the front porch lost its function as a place to greet people walking along the street. The ranch was set back from the road, and picture window allowed the family to watch the traffic. Families after World War II moved from the front porch to the backyard, where they built a patio or deck, installed a charcoal grill and valued the quiet and privacy that the backyard provided.

Building all of the rooms on one level reduced construction costs. The walls of a single story bore less weight, and space and material consuming stairwells were not required. The house was often built on a slab foundation. Rooms were small in a typically 1500 square feet house. The split level is an upscale modification of the ranch. The central core contain kitchen and central living room and is flanked by a lower level isolating the garage and perhaps an informal family room and children's play area. On the other side of the core, an upper level isolates quiet bedrooms and bath.

Manufactured housing, also known as mobile home or trailer, is the newest addition to the housing landscape in western New York. According to the 1990 census, about 15 per cent of local housing units in Allegany County are mobile homes, typical of rural counties in the United States. Many units are

170 years ago, the owners of this house sat on their front porch to greet their Whitesville neighbors. Over the generations, dormers were added on the second floor and a new kitchen was built at the rear. Now the wooden deck at the right, far from the road, is the center of family activity when weather permits (author's photo).

located in mobile home parks built just outside of village limits, where zoning restrictions do not apply and property taxes are lower. Yet, residents have easy access to post office, school and other village services.

Several advantages of mobile homes help to explain their popularity as a housing choice. The cost per square foot of trailers is typically about half the cost of a site built home, an important consideration for low-income families. Median household income in Allegany County in 1997 was $31,291, about $5000 below the New York State median income. Eighteen per cent of Allegany County residents live below the poverty level. Nationally, the median income of manufactured housing residents is $22,600, compared to $31,400 for households living in site built housing (Dream Home or Nightmare? 1988). Living in a trailer with a monthly rental or mortgage/property tax/insurance payment of $400 per month holds family housing costs to about 25 per cent of family income.

Trailers may be small, but less square footage may be suitable for small households. And the modern household is smaller. In 2000, the census reports that the average Allegany County household contains 2.5 persons. One in four Allegany County residents live in a one person household in 2000. A trailer provides adequate space for a 24-year-old single person living alone, or a

This small trailer provides affordable housing for a small household, is renter occupied, is situated on a small lot close to the road, and has similar trailers as close neighbors on either side (author's photo).

retired spouse whose spouse has died. About one-fifth of households are composed of a retired couple whose grown children are living on their own or newly wed couple just starting out (O'Hare and O'Hare 1993).

The availability of trailer housing also increases the options available to women in contemporary Allegany County. Women now fully participate in the work force, although in disproportionately low-wage jobs. Earning their own income and having low cost trailer housing available enables them to provide for their children and avoid or escape a bad marriage. Females head 13 percent of Allegany households in 2000.

Quality of mobile home construction has also improved in recent decades. Federal regulations since 1974 have mandated higher standards for fire proofing, insulation and anchoring. Today's doublewide mobile home is likely to have two baths, sometimes three bedrooms and amenities like a picture window. Once a mobile home is placed on a site, it is unlikely to ever move again, particularly for the one-half of trailer owners who own the land on which their home sits. Owners often add to the sense of permanence by hiding the absence of a foundation and basement with skirting, landscaping and an entrance porch.

Choosing a trailer for low cost housing also frees up family income for other purchases, such as satellite dish, sports utility vehicle, home com-

For this manufactured home, the carefully tended shrubbery, ample windows, large lot and trees convey a sense of permanence and good living (author's photo).

puter or snowmobile. In Victorian days, most of the opportunities for conspicuous consumption were related to the home. In the automobile and information ages, the home is no longer the principal indicator of social status. Households have many more consumption alternatives than they did in 1890.

Trailers also provide the rewards of home ownership to low-income households. Nearly three-quarters of Allegany County residents in 2000 own the housing they live in, compared to just over half for the New York State average. Monthly mortgage payments are deductible from earned income in calculating federal and state tax. Long-term mortgage loans are now available on good quality manufactured housing, which lowers monthly payments. Also, owing to village zoning regulations, most manufactured housing units are located along the ribbon highways that connect villages, not in the villages themselves. Rural residents still pay town, county and school taxes on the value of their property, but not being liable to village taxation reduces their local tax bill by one third.

Trailers do have disadvantages. They are smaller, typically having about 80 percent of the floor space of a modest site built home. With no basement or attic space, a storage shed is a frequent addition to the mobile home property. And like owners of small site built homes, owners of trailers

This household has added a picture window and an entrance porch and two late model cars are parked at the far right. Over the past decade, the owner replaced the original aerial for TV reception with a large satellite dish and later with a small dish to its left (author's photo).

The owners of this trailer have added rooms on both front and rear. Some additional household income went to purchase the boat, whose bow protrudes from behind the house (author's photo).

sometimes build additions to increase usable space. Trailers, like automobiles, depreciate over time, while a well constructed site built house often appreciates in value over time. One survey of 1,029 mobile home owners reports that two-thirds believe that their trailer would sell for less than the paid for their home (Dream Home or Nightmare? 1988). Concern that manufactured housing will depreciate in value over time is one reason why banks charge a higher interest rate to purchase a trailer than to buy a conventional site built house.

Other community members sometimes attach a certain stigma to residents who live in trailers (Hecht 1998; Moon and Rollison 1998). Trailer residents were not only poor, but the very concept of trailer or mobile home conveyed a sense of impermanence and social marginality in the community that invited comparison to the much despised wandering gypsies of Europe (Hill 1999). Of course, many residents of manufactured homes are well integrated into the community. They are permanent residents, attend school functions, belong to a church or social club and visit local friends and relatives. Trailers are generally not a stylish form of vernacular housing, but they are the best available housing alternative for many low-income households.

In wealthier suburban areas, housing tastes have rejected low-slung horizontal ranches in favor of large, two-story mansionettes featuring Palladian windows, complex roof lines, and a double story great room. Irregular roof lines and footprints get away from the box-like quality of ranches and manufactured housing and add visual interest (Langdon 1987). Size of home and lot are valuable indicators of social status, and families own more space consuming possessions. Investing in expensive housing is attractive during a long period of low interest rates, and the federal government gives favorable tax treatment to mortgage interest payments. Family attention has turned inward, and each family member has their own private room fully equipped with a personal computer and the latest electronic gear. Mansionettes are the preferred style in suburban America, but few are being constructed in the villages of western New York. The population of the house building 25–45 year age bracket is declining, and incomes are lagging behind.

The counties of western New York prospered at the end of the nineteenth century, and the attractive Victorian era housing stock in commercial villages reflect that prosperity. What are contemporary owners to do with the spacious nineteenth century Queen Anne houses? Some are carved up into multiple apartments; many large older homes now have multiple gas meters attached to the side and several mailboxes flank the front door. Some have been converted into bed and breakfasts. Others now house travel agent, law office, and other small businesses.

LOCAL POLITICAL ISSUES IN A LARGER SOCIETY

The political center of New York is the heavily populated, narrow corridor along the Erie Canal and New York State throughway connecting New York City and Buffalo. A rural dominated state legislature once shaped the distribution of taxing and spending; today urban and suburban areas are more likely to define state priorities (Luloff and Swanson 1990).

In 1840, Allegany County had 40,000 residents, 1.7 percent of New York State's total population. Over the next 160 years, Allegany population added only 10,000 more residents, while the state population increased seven-fold. From 1840 to 1940, while Allegany County population held constant, urban Erie County (Buffalo) increased 12-fold and Monroe County (Rochester) grew by a factor of six. At the national level, the political center shifts west and south; New York State loses electoral votes each decade. Western New York lost one seat in the post 2000 Congressional redistricting and the former 31st Congressional District that extended from Elmira to Jamestown was carved up between more heavily populated areas in Buffalo and Rochester.

The way Republicans and Democrats choose their presidential candidates has sharpened partisan conflict since the cultural upheaval of the Vietnam War in the late 1960s. Before Vietnam, professional politicians selected presidential candidates, and they preferred to select nominees who would be acceptable to party rank and file members and appeal to centrist independent voters not firmly aligned with either party as well. This practice promoted moderation and compromise, as both Republican and Democratic parties leaned toward the center on policy issues. In the post Vietnam years, rank and file party members have selected presidential candidates by voting in presidential primaries. Primary voters tend to be committed to the ideals and platforms of their party, and they prefer candidates who are strong supporters of party ideology. The primary election process sharpens differences between the parties and has polarized politics, particularly since the election of Republican Ronald Reagan in 1980 (Sundquist 1983, p. 330).

Republican values of limited government and low taxes, the authority of church and government in regulating individual behavior, and family oriented social values continue to appeal to an Allegany County majority. As we have seen in previous chapters, the moral issues of slavery, prohibition and nativism have always led a majority of Allegany voters to vote Republican. Today these moral values are expressed in opposition to abortion and the sanctity of marriage between man and woman (Green, Rozell and Wilcox 2003, p. 9). New evangelical churches built on low cost land along rural roads are thriving, while main line Protestant churches in small villages struggle.

The 2002 election for governor, won by Republican George Pataki, suggests that the continued strong position of the Republican Party among Allegany County voters reflects mistrust of big state government in Albany rather than social conservatism or the civil war tradition. The independent campaign of Thomas Golisano, a very successful small business owner from upstate, championed smaller government run more efficiently. He won more votes in Allegany County than Democrat Carl McCall, an African- American associated with the downstate Democratic Party. While many Allegany County residents are socially conservative, in 2002 Golisano's small government campaign swamped the Right to Life Party, which received only 196 votes in the entire county.

Friends and neighbors politics are alive and well to the present day, especially within primary politics within the dominant Republican Party. In a representative race for Republican nomination for County Clerk in 2003, the winner polled 55 percent of the county vote, winning by two to one majorities in several towns and losing by the same margin in others. Local party leaders were able to urge their supporters to the polls out of personal loyalty rather than position on issues or quality of the incumbent's performance.

Declining transportation costs and increasing economies of scale have changed the important local political issues of the day. Two hundred years ago, the poor condition of roads meant that the frontier settler relied entirely upon his immediate neighbors, a village about four miles away, and a town government to provide goods and services that the farm family could not provide itself. In 1806, when a horse and wagon could negotiate rough trails with difficulty, the Allegany County settler rarely ventured further than the nearest town, four miles from the farm, a tiring trip that would take the better part of a day. Every farm in Allegany County was located close to church, school, general store and town government that provided needed services. Improving roads was critical, and by 1840 county legislators attempted to tax county residents one or two days of labor per year to fill holes, maintain ditches and build up the crown of the road to permit surface water to run off. No doubt many citizens agreed that improving roads was a good thing, yet they often did their best to avoid the labor tax the county government tried to impose.

Now, 200 years later, Allegany County residents are closely linked to national institutions that provide services. We can easily fly 2000 miles in a day, or drive to Rochester and return in one day. The cars we buy are manufactured in Kentucky, the television programs we watch are produced in New York, and our clothes are made in China or Honduras and are bought at Wal-Mart which is headquartered in Arkansas. This process of centralization raises many important political issues in Allegany County. Two centuries later, three major political issues dominate local political discussion in Allegany County.

The classic county court house, built in 1936, incorporates Greek and Roman architectural ideas, symbolizing democracy and the rule of law. County government seeks a just and well ordered society, and local voters hold elected officials responsible for their actions (Allegany County Historian).

These issues are county taxing and spending, school centralization and waste disposal services.

Sample county budgets in Table 7.5 show taxing and spending trends over a 25-year period.

In both 1978 and 2002, health and human services account for two-thirds of county spending. In real terms, after adjusting for inflation, county spending was about the same in 1978 and 2002. But the burden on local taxpayers was greater in 2002. In 1978, the county received 60.8 percent of its revenues from state and local governments, but in 2002 state and federal assistance had shrunk to 43.7 percent of the county budget. To make up the difference, legislators now require county agencies to charge for some services that were provided free to the user in 1978. Legislators have also had to double the real property tax rate. Raising this highly visible tax is politically difficult. But it is the only tax available to legislators, who can raise the revenue required to fund the annual budget simply by adjusting the tax rate. Taxpayer resistance to rising property tax bills probably explains why Allegany County citizens gave 22 percent of their votes to Independent Thomas Golisano in the 2002 gubernatorial race.

Allegany County voters appreciate the valuable services that county government provides—public safety, road maintenance and social services for

Table 7.5.   Taxing and Spending in Allegany County, 1978 and 2002

	1978		2002	
Spending Category	$(000)	%	$(000)	%
General Government Support	1876	10.0	5706	9.3
Social Services	11624	62.9	33344	54.4
Health	1001	5.4	7542	12.3
Public Safety	576	3.1	5150	8.4
Highways	3270	17.5	6775	11.1
Other	363	1.1	2768	4.5
Total	18710	100.0	61285	100.0
Revenue Categories				
Real Property Tax	2565	13.7	14995	24.5
Non Property Tax	3755	20.1	592	9.7
State Aid	4200	22.4	11851	19.3
Federal Aid	7191	38.4	14383	23.4
Other Revenues	999	5.3	14131	23.1
Total	18710	99.9	61285	100.0

Source: Allegany County Board of Legislators Proceedings, 1878 and 2002. Internal Transfers are omitted.

needy children and the elderly. County employees who provide these services are also strong advocates for more spending. In its 2002 annual report, Social Services, the largest department, noted that they provided over 10,000 families with food stamps, Medicaid and child and family services. And the agency argues that county taxpayers get a very good deal: Social Services expends only $810 per family in county tax dollars to serve these 10,200 families while bringing into the county $3,587 per family in revenues from state and federal governments.

The local political consequences of state mandates are mixed. On the one hand, state and federal funds provides services for county residents, and creates jobs for health care workers, landfill and road employees and sheriff deputies. But county legislators know that the $810 cost to serve an additional family must be raised through an increase in property taxes, and the Commissioner of Social Services acknowledges the difficulty of "balancing the sometimes conflicting needs of providing important services and minimizing expenditure" (Proceedings of the Board of Legislators of Allegany County 2002). And their taxpayers resent having to pay the taxes to support social services. A large property tax bill paid once a year is painfully obvious to the taxpayer, and other people seem to be principal beneficiaries. The taxpayer senses that they pay their full share, but receive only part of the goods and services that local governments provide.

Local voters also resent that state government in Albany requires local governments to provide psychological counseling in the schools, establish recycling programs as part of solid waste management, and pay for essential medical services for low income families. New York State mandates that local governments meet uniform standards in the services they provide. Counties cannot reduce the local property tax by stiffening Medicaid eligibility requirements, or cutting back on employee fringe benefits, or modifying landfill operating practice or changing the design specifications for a lightly used county bridge (Gold and Ritchie 1994).

Why do state legislators impose mandates on county government that raise the ire of local taxpayers? State legislators are quick to provide generous Medicaid services to low-income populations because these legislators need pick up only 25 percent of the tab. The federal government pays one-half of the total cost, and the state requires that local governments pay 25 percent. The local share of Medicaid costs increases faster than the revenues generated from sales and property taxes. State regulations also limit the number of prisoners held in county jail to prevent overcrowding. When the number of prisoners increases beyond prison capacity, county government must release prisoners prematurely or rent prison cell space from neighboring jurisdictions, at considerable additional cost.

Replacing small local schools with larger centralized schools is the second recurrent issue. Larger K-12 schools with more pupils can provide a wider range of services at lower per pupil cost. The 1855 Census recorded 258 schools, an average of nine schools per six square mile town. Most pupils lived within a mile of their one room school. New York State began to promote school consolidation in the 1930s and 1940s as roads improved and the spread of the automobile reduced the burden of travel from farm to central school. In 1938, for example, Fillmore and 27 adjoining school districts voted to consolidate and in 1940 the Alfred and Almond school districts merged. Today, ten public school systems serve Allegany County school children and more merger discussions are underway.

The purpose of consolidation is to provide a stronger, more varied education at lower cost per student. Larger schools can employ a guidance counselor, teach foreign languages, buy science laboratory equipment and computers, and field interscholastic sports teams. But many villages fight to keep their local school, valuing close personal attention to their students and better opportunities to play on the soccer team or work on the yearbook. Community residents also value the school as a center of community activity and fear that loss of a school will make the community a less attractive place to live. Furthermore, school centralization might erode property values, as newcomers to the county will settle in the larger village where the school is located and will be willing to pay less for housing in villages without a school. And, rather than walking ten minutes to school,

The boys play baseball and the girls play ring around the rosy during recess at this classic one room school house at Five Corners, town of Alfred, around 1880 (Hinkle Library, Alfred State College).

their sons and daughters will have to ride 30 minutes on the yellow school bus.

New York State actively encourages local schools to consolidate. They offer the carrot of increased financial aid to school districts that consolidate. And they use the stick of requiring that all school districts provide expensive educational programs. Advocates of consolidation believe that Allegany County schools have been slow to consolidate, and that ultimately all small schools with about 400 students in grades K–12 should be merged into a few large regional schools.

The third major issue in Allegany politics is whether the county should offer waste disposal services in exchange for cash payments from waste disposal companies. The county's low population density and low land costs enable the county to consider offering waste disposal services and to apply the tipping fees received to lower property taxes, improve services, and create jobs. Opponents fear that waste will eventually leak into the environment, threatening the health and well being of present and future generations. Waste dump imagery is inconsistent with the image of a clean, uncrowded and pristine landscape that makes living in Allegany County pleasurable to many.

The one room school house gave way to this large consolidated central school like this one in Scio where about 100 students and staff are pictured. School consolidation accelerated with automobile ownership and improved roads beginning in the 1930s (Allegany County Historian).

County public opinion has strongly opposed tying Allegany County's economic future to being a trash bin for urban waste. County legislators have consistently refused to sell space in the state of the art county solid waste landfill. Their constituents do not want to risk contamination associated with storing New York City's garbage, or speed the day when a new landfill must be sited and built in some Allegany County residents' back yard (Rasmussen 1990).

In the case of the Hyland landfill in Angelica, the company offered the people of Angelica a substantial monetary payment in exchange for the community bearing the inconvenience of having a nuisance project in the community and the risk of groundwater pollution leaking into the local water supply. The town of Angelica is evenly split over the continued operation of the Hyland landfill project. Some voters value a cash cow that funds 89 percent of the Angelica town budget. Opponents argue that the landfill will eventually leak, and that the present generation should not impose health risks on future generations.

Opposition to waste disposal projects has been carried to the streets on several occasions. Public protest led to closing down a waste to energy incinerator in Cuba in 1992. The public battle against a New York State proposal to store low-level radioactive waste in Allegany County revealed the depth of local suspicion of New York State and the depth of local resistance to the idea of trashing the local environment.

The story began in 1988, when New York State created a special siting commission to locate sites to store low level radioactive waste generated in hospitals and nuclear power plants. The siting commission clumsily decreed that Allegany County, meeting basic geological and demographic character-istics, was likely to be selected. Allegany County residents, organized as the Concerned Citizens of Allegany County (CCAC), waged an effective non-vi-olent protest campaign (Peterson 2001). Over a 15-month period, many protest meetings were held, the credibility of the siting commission attacked, and non violent protesters arrested for interfering with siting commission activities.

In April 1990, Governor Mario Cuomo announced that New York State would no longer consider sites in Allegany County. The discredited siting commission was soon disbanded. New York State has continued to search for a low-level radioactive waste storage site within the state as an alternative to onsite storage at the nuclear power plants that generate most of the waste. On-site storage at nuclear plants located on major lakes and rivers is not suitable. New York State has belatedly addressed local health and safety concerns and enriched compensation packages to host communities, but this complex issue has not yet been resolved. However, owing to the spirited, effective protest activities of many residents, Allegany County will not be part of the solution.

The citizens of Allegany County have ensured that the federal government will not be empowered to force a county like Allegany to accept low-level ra-dioactive waste. A 1985 federal law requires states to join an interstate com-pact or to provide for the storage of low-level radioactive waste themselves. New York State filed a lawsuit in federal court, largely at the behest of Alle-gany County citizens, claiming that the 1985 law violated the Tenth Amend-ment to the constitution, which protects states' rights. The Supreme Court de-cided in favor of New York State by a 6 to 3 vote in June 1992.

THE CHANGING LANDSCAPE: FROM PASTURE TO FOREST

Today the forest has filled out the landscape, 200 years after first generation settlers cleared the original trees. Then as now the distribution of tree species in any local ecosystem is determined by whether slopes faced north or south, the wetness of the soil and whether fire had recently visited the ecosystem. Originally, large quadrupeds like elk, wolves and bear flourished, but by 1900 they had largely disappeared owing to loss of habitat and hostility of their human enemies. Populations of bear and coyote are now expanding as habitat is restored. Abundant abandoned pasture land also favors species that flourish at the forest edge, such as song birds, fox, woodchucks, raccoons, skunks and opossum (Whitney 1944).

By the early twentieth century, the conversion of forest to pasture was complete, farmers keeping about 20 percent of their land in forest to provide firewood, fence posts, habitat for deer and a place of refuge. The absent forest signified local agricultural prosperity. One-hundred years later, forest has reclaimed the pastures of western New York as the dairy industry has steadily declined (McKibben 1995). The pasture grasses of a recently abandoned field are joined by shrubs that can withstand grazing animals. Later, small birds and animals drop seeds that sprout into oaks, beeches and conifers, and the wind blows in the winged seeds of maples. Today, although the trees have reclaimed the land once again, most western New Yorkers barely notice their environment as they whiz through it at 60 miles an hour on their way to work, to the store where they shop, and to the place where they play. They purchase the food that an earlier generation grew. In our material society, we pay less attention to our local environment and focus more on the money we earn as producers and the goods we buy as consumers. Most Allegany County residents neither fear their environment nor celebrate its quiet beauty; the forested environment seems less relevant for daily lives. Most of us pay little attention to the forested landscape that today surrounds our villages and we rarely venture into the woods.

But if one ventures to walk along the Allegany County portion of the Finger Lakes Trail, part of an 800 mile system of trails extending from Buffalo and Allegany State Forest in the west to the Catskills in the east, one can appreciate a changing intricate ecosystem (fltc@frontiernet.net). Along the trail, one sees signs of the glaciers that shaped the landscape 8,000 years ago, variation in the trees that grow depending upon elevations and moisture, and signs of past human habitation (Wessels 1977).

About 9,000 years ago, the glaciers had retreated and pine, oak and birch forest populations were established on the warming land. Two-hundred years ago, a generation of settlers transformed the mature forest into cropland and pasture. Over the past century, the forested landscape has been restored as the dairy industry in western New York has declined. When the State of New York bought the lands of bankrupt dairy farmers in the 1930s, they planted some fields in red pine but, owing to lack of funds, left other fields to regenerate on their own. Today, the fields that were left to regenerate on their own are a richer and more varied ecosystem. Seedlings from many different plant species sprout, and the ones best suited to its square yard microenvironment generally succeed. These mixed forests produce more wooded material from

This folk artist has integrated home into its surrounding environment. Grass grows along the foundation, vines trail around the windows, spectacular flowers grace the wall. The house has cut the view of the pine tree in half, and the artist has apologized by adding the trunk visually (author's photo).

the sun's energy, have richer soils and support varied insect, bird and small mammal populations in diverse habitats (Heinrich 1997).

Today, black cherry and red oak are the most valuable commercial hardwoods. The red pine planted on state lands in the 1930s is used primarily for pulp and paper. Local sawmills also convert some red pine into construction materials. Commercial foresters ignore pasture trees which typically sprout multiple branches from the main trunk during their years of rapid growth. The knots that form weaken the lumber and are often not pleasing to the customer's eye. Trees that have grown 16 feet tall before a major fork forms are the most commercially valuable. As these trees grew, they put their energy to growing upward toward the sun in competition with other trees.

The New York State Department of Environmental Conservation (DEC) manages state forest land. DEC responsibilities include forest thinning and harvesting as well as trail maintenance and development, but manpower shortages inhibit their work. DEC recommends assignment of one forester per 10,000 acres of state land. Allegany County has 50,000 acres of state land, and only two foresters; in the 1970s, 14 foresters were employed to manage state forest land (NYS DEC Allegany County 2005).

After 200 years of human settlement, today's forests contain smaller trees and higher tree densities than did forests in 1806 (Leahy and Pregitzer 2003). The distribution of tree species in any local ecosystem is determined by whether slopes face north or south, the wetness of the soil, and whether fire has recently visited the ecosystem. Beech, hemlocks and sugar maples, being shade tolerant, do well in the deep forest. Check the ground cover in forest where minimal light reaches the forest floor to find an under story dominated by these trees. Oaks, ash, basswood and hickories do better along the sunny edge of fields and where gaps in the forest canopy allow strong light to reach the small trees. Red oak, which has a strong root system and leathery leaves that resist desiccation, does well on dry, wind exposed ridges. During long periods of above average rainfall, yellow birch is likely to thrive while beech flourishes on drier sites that expand when rainfall is below normal.

Tree species need to protect themselves from the warming effect of the winter sun. When the bark warms on a sunny winter day its bark expands followed by contraction during the cold winter night. That expansion and contraction can damage the surface of the tree, in the same way that thawing and freezing accelerates formation of potholes in our roads in the late winter. Light colored bark reflects light, protecting beech trees from the winter sun. Heavy rough bark of a hickory tree is a different protective adaptation (Wessels 1977).

Trees grow to maximize the amount of sunlight they can capture. The sunlight is the energy source that enables the tree to convert chlorophyll, the green in the leaves, into food. Notice how trees maximize the exposure of their leaves to the sun. To capture the sun's rays, a tree's topmost branches stretch upward, its middle branches grow outward and low branches grow downward. Individual trees will also tilt toward the sun and away from a shade producing neighbor that monopolizes the sunlight (Oliver and Larson 1966).

Whether an individual tree grows alone or has many neighbors determines the shape of an individual tree. All trees grow to maximize their exposure to sunlight, source of the energy that transforms chlorophyll into the tree's woody material. Individual trees will grow at an angle away from neighbors to maximize the sunlight that reaches their leaves. When a tree grows in a field alone, it sends heavy limbs outward from its trunk to capture the most sun. Farmers often leave a tree in their pasture to provide shade for their animals. Pasture trees typically have large bushy canopies. Today, deep in the forest, you can spot large pasture trees along field boundaries marked by large trees and rock walls.

A few Allegany County trees escaped the woodsman's axe, surviving to be more than a century old. They are most likely to be found in low-lying valleys distant from roads and streams. In remote locations, cutting an access road and hauling the felled trees uphill was too time-consuming for the woodsman (Kershner 1995). Old trees have scars on the trunk where large branches broke off in the distant past. In general, the larger the diameter of a tree, the greater its age; large diameter is also related to growing conditions. The oldest trees we are likely to see are pasture trees, left by farmers to provide shade for their grazing animals and now surrounded by young trees that have taken over abandoned pastures. Very few large, old deciduous trees have escaped the eager eye of lumbermen seeking logs for nearby saw mills.

When a pasture is abandoned, as has happened throughout western New York since the 1930s, young beech, oak and maple seedlings compete with each other to capture the sun's rays. Their most successful strategy is to grow fast and straight upward. Their strength goes to growing tall and their canopy is quite small compared to a pasture tree of the same species. The fields that farmers abandoned about 30–50 years ago today are dominated by straight, tall trees with small canopies. Frequently, one species will dominate a field. They took hold during a mast year, when the parent tree produced many seeds to ensure that predators could not consume all of the seeds produced.

Early settlers in the town of Almond assembled the stone fence, probably around 1820. The fence protected the two large maple trees, which grew into large trees that were harvested about 1920. From the two stumps, two shoots have grown to the present large trees. The pasture in the background was probably abandoned about the 1950s. The saplings grow straight and tall, competing with neighboring saplings for access to the suns rays (author's photo).

A walk in the forest reveals signs of farms abandoned with the twentieth century decline of the dairy industry. Field stone tossed into piles indicates that the farmer was planting corn and other crops. Early every spring, limestone deposited by the glaciers 10,000 years ago is heaved upward to the soil surface by the daily cycle of freezing and thawing. Left in place, these stones would interfere with farm machinery and reduce yields per acre. Field stone stacked neatly into fences reveals that the land was used for pasture, and the fence kept farm animals in a pasture or out of a field of row crops or hay.

Invention of barbed wire in the 1870 replaced the laborious construction of stone fences (Wessels 1977). Strands of barbed wire also indicate the boundaries of now abandoned fields. The animals were kept on the side of the tree where the barbed wire is attached. Should the cattle push against the fence, they would push the barbed wire into the tree and strengthen the fence. Sharp eyed observers can locate the stone foundations of long abandoned farm houses and barns. To find the original house, look for privet, apple trees, a lilac bush, perennial flowers and ground cover, or old milk containers. The stone foundations are often close to a secondary road that today provides access to hunting cabins and seasonal residences.

This farm site along the Finger Lakes Trail in the town of Almond was abandoned during the 1930s when the State of New York bought out hard pressed farmers. One remaining wall of the foundation still stands, behind the milk can. Trees grow in what was formerly the cellar (author's photo).

By 1900, farmers had converted forest to pasture to such an extent that the deer population was much reduced. Nationally, the deer population in the United States is estimated at one-million in 1900, compared to 18-million deer today when field has reverted back to forest, providing ample cover for the deer population. Every year, thousands of hunters visit their favorite Allegany County sites, and deer hunting contributes to the local economy. Deer hunters from Rochester and Buffalo buy land, build cabins and pay property taxes. They fill motel rooms, shop in stores, and eat restaurant meals (Patterson n.d.). Venison and deerskin apparel supplement household incomes, and hunting is a pleasurable recreational activity. Allegany is among the leading New York State counties in the annual take by deer hunters.

Of course, prolific deer populations impose costs too. Every time a car collides with a deer crossing a road, average damage to the car is $2,000. Roughly 720 deer/vehicle collisions happen in Allegany County in a typical year, causing about $1.4-million in damage to cars. The hungry deer population decimates shrubbery every winter, and cuts into garden crop yields during the summer. New York State figures suggest that agricultural damage is about 60 percent of vehicle damage, or about $880 million (dec.state.ny/deer; Insurance Information Institute). Deer also alter the understory of our forests. They prefer to browse on young ash and oak shoots and don't care to eat beech trees and ferns.

Hunting is an important tool to manage deer population size. How long this approach will work is uncertain to the extent that children of hunters are not inclined to continue the family hunting tradition. One alternative is to treat deer as pests and to take more aggressive steps to reduce their numbers. For example, the hunting season could be extended or hunting could be legal all year. That would reduce the deer population, but it would also endanger non-hunters hiking in the woods. In a recent year, 27 accidental shootings occurred in the four county Southern Tier. Or society can let deer population increase (and increase shrubbery nibbling and road crossings) and then die in large numbers during harsh winters and during periods of low food supply.

In 2006, the forest permits landowners to turn trees into cash, and deer hunting contributes to the local economy every fall. Hunting is today more recreational than an essential food gathering activity, and local hunters are declining in number. Hunting is less important as an income supplement and must compete with other forms of recreation. Most Allegany County residents define the economic impact of deer as their predations on household shrubbery and damage to automobiles from untimely road crossings.

TODAY'S ECONOMIC CHALLENGES AND OPPORTUNITIES

The challenges of promoting economic growth in western New York are considerable. The logic of transportation costs and economies of scale does not work to the advantage of western New York communities. People prefer not to live a long distance from where they work, shop and play, and that argues for the continuing decline of small villages that were economic centers 200 years ago. And larger metropolitan areas across the nation may continue to siphon off population from western New York. Retailers like Wal-Mart and McDonalds can serve western New York markets profitably and put smaller mom-and-pop jewelers, bakeries and restaurants out of business. Manufacturing firms who need access to specialized office serices, marketing and financial services are likely to locate in metropolitan areas where such services are close at hand. Specialized retail entrepreneurs—coffee shops, sporting goods stores and orthodontists—will also locate in metropolitan areas to access more consumers with higher incomes.

The weakness of New York State's economy, and especially the troubles of Rochester and Buffalo, makes it harder for rural counties like Allegany to thrive. High taxes, New York's taxes being one-third higher than the national average, are one reason for economic decline in New York State since World War II. Air conditioning has made the American South a much more attractive place to live. High labor costs have caused loss of jobs in New York, particularly in the manufacturing sector. Factories first moved to the South and later to off-shore locations in Mexico and China. This broad trend in manufacturing decline has hit rural counties particularly hard; many of the small niche factories that flourished around 1900 in the villages of Allegany County closed their doors after World War II.

However, rural western New York counties may be able to rebound. One possibility is that traditional industries, oil production and agriculture, may lead an economic revival. Oil prices are certain to rise, and the wells that were capped in the 1990s may resume production. Will oil prices rise to a point where local producers will begin production again? If the transition to renewable energy production is rapid and the increase in demand for petroleum slows, oil production in western New York may never resume. A revival of agriculture may be possible. Demand for agricultural products will certainly increase, given growing and wealthier world populations and the quest to fuel automobiles with vegetable oil and corn rather than petroleum. Research to develop seeds that mature more quickly or tolerate frost could lead to the revival of agriculture in Allegany County.

Better transportation is essential to any economic revival. The closing of the railroad after World War II spelled economic disaster for Allegany

County. The interstate highway system that replaced the train bypassed Allegany County, with east west interstate traffic passing through the Erie Canal corridor and through central Pennsylvania. With completion of Interstate 86 through the Southern Tier, the playing field will be level once again, as commerce and industry may consider locating in Allegany County to take advantage of low land costs and good schools and public services. Local communities and the county must provide water and sewer hookups if they hope to attract new business.

Today, well organized local government is needed to provide essential services at reasonable cost to taxpayers. Towns created 200 years ago on the frontier continue unchanged 200 years later. Joseph Ellicott originally drew the six square mile town boundaries to identify with precision the location of the lands that settlers purchased. Ellicott's town system was an artificial grid imposed upon the 3.3 million acres of wilderness owned by the Holland Land Company. Ellicott's land surveyors drew precise town boundaries and lot lines that minimized controversies over land ownership. Later, towns were a convenient size for local government to provide essential services like maintaining roads and settling legal disputes at a time when the county seat in Belmont was a long journey over rough roads. Have the original town governments outlived their usefulness as county and state governments provide more services? Should road maintenance and resolution of misdemeanor cases continue to be provided at the town level?

Certainly town governments are familiar to county residents and are regarded with affection. Residents know their elected town supervisors and employees and know they will provide good quality local services. At least 15 local residents donate their time to serve on the elected town boards and on appointed boards of assessment review and zoning appeal. But the services that towns provide are expensive. In 2004, a typical town spends about $500,000 of which two-thirds is spent on road maintenance in the summer and snow plowing in the winter. A town will employ four full-time employees and operates perhaps four dump trucks, a grader, a front loader and several other pieces of capital equipment. Together, the 29 towns spend nearly $15 million to provide essential services.

County government could provide about the same level of service at lower cost. No doubt in a severe snow storm, more workers and equipment will be clearing roads when towns are responsible. But on a weekly basis, workers and equipment will have less idle time if the county organized snow removal efforts. Towns once provided some solid waste collection locally but the county now uses only seven transfer stations, not 29, to provide a convenient drop off point for county residents. Perhaps that model would be appropriate for decentralizing workers and equipment dedicated to road maintenance.

The current trend toward decentralization of business may work to Allegany County's advantage. Rural areas have gained from a wave of decentralized, computer-based information processing investment, and high tech investments require a large, well-trained labor force (Glasmier 1991). Computers and internet communication reduces the advantage to companies of locating near their customer base, a major factor in urban growth (Freshwater 1998). Now billing services and toll free long distance telephone services can be located anywhere. With email, workers can communicate with each other without being in physical proximity. The home based virtual office is challenging the real office where dozens of workers physically work in the same building. The death of distance (Cairncross 1997) requires substantial infrastructure investment, and so far the most successful rural areas are located close to metropolitan centers (Glasmier 1991). More cell phone towers are required to provide adequate service in hilly areas, and high speed internet access is essential.

Western New York communities will face stiff competition from rural areas in the Sunbelt states where population is growing rapidly. Nationwide, population in two-thirds of non metropolitan counties is increasing. Of those counties that are growing, about 75 percent have large employers such as universities, state prisons and large manufacturers; are near to metropolitan suburbs; or have strong retirement and recreational potential. Counties with warm weather, low cost of land to support golf course, swimming pool and low density housing appeal to retirees. These counties also attract younger families who fill service related jobs created by retirees and for whom warm weather is equally appealing. The most successful counties are Sunbelt counties that attract retirees and counties that are close to metropolitan areas where commuters build bedroom communities. Across America, one-third of all rural counties captured over three-quarters of all rural economic gains during the 1990s (Drabenstott 2000). For ex-farming counties like Allegany, it is difficult to compete with these rural counties (Johnson and Beale 1995).

The Allegany County economy struggles to export goods and services outside of the county. Outsiders used to purchase dairy products from Allegany County, and manufacturing sales were substantial. Today Allegany County's largest export is higher education. Meanwhile, Allegany County residents spend a large percentage of their incomes outside the county on leisure travel to cities and warmer climates, communication and entertainment that originates in New York and Los Angeles, food grown in the Midwest and California, and manufacturing products produced all over the world (Newman 1972).

For 150 years, people have moved from the farms to villages and metropolitan areas to benefit from lower transportation costs and economies of scale available in larger cities. Initially, the benefits from dairy production were widely distributed, but a resource drain of capital and especially labor has accompanied the demise of dairy in western New York. Today, the question is whether creation of high paying jobs can reverse the loss of the productive 25–49 age group. The market has largely bypassed western New York. It is possible that the advantages of centralization will wane in the age of computers and advanced telecommunications technology.

Investment opportunities to build prisons and solid waste storage facilities exist, but there is no consensus that the economic benefits are positive (Besser and Hanson 2004), or that the risks to community health and safety are worth bearing. Rural land use planning is needed to preserve the visual integrity, and seasonal recreational opportunities in the heavily populated portions of the county, while developing prisons, landfills, and similar nuisance projects in remote areas of the county. The rates charged for providing these socially valuable services would have to be high enough to compensate private land owners fairly and to provide revenue to the county for infrastructure development and tax reduction. However, in recent decades, county residents have been unwilling to pay these costs. Many believe the neighborly intimacy of small communities where neighbors need not lock their doors is at risk. The benefits of economic growth may not be worth the social costs imposed upon rural communities.

Bibliography

Adams, Margaret Byrd. 2004. *American Wood Heat Cookery.* Seattle: Pacific Search Press. Third edition, Alfred: Marrasm Press.

Allen, Leonard L. 1934. *History of the New York State Grange.* Watertown: Hungerford Holbrook.

Aquila, Richard. 1983. *The Iroquois Restoration.* Detroit: Wayne State University Press.

Ashworth, John. 1983. *Agrarians and Aristocrats Agrarians: Party Political Ideology in the United States, 1837–1846.* Atlantic Highlands, NJ: Humanities Press Inc.

Axelrod, Robert. 1984. *The Evolution of Cooperation.* New York: Basic Books.

Baker, Paula. 1991. *The Moral Frameworks of Public Life: Gender, Politics and the State in Rural New York.* New York: Oxford University Press.

Barboza, David. 2001. Cheese State Fights to Stay That Way. *New York Times*, June 28, p. A 1.

Barron, Hal S. 1997. *Mixed Harvest: The Second Great Transformation in the Rural North 1870–1930.* Raleigh: University of North Carolina Press.

———. 1984. *Those Who Stayed Behind: Rural Society in 19th Century New England.* Cambridge: Cambridge University Press.

Bateman, Fred. 1968. Improvement in American Dairy Farming, 1850–1910: A Quantitative Analysis. *Journal of Economic History*, Vol. 28, June.

———. 1969. Labor Inputs and Productivity in American Dairy Agriculture, 1850–1910. *Journal of Economic History*, Vol. 29, June.

Beers, D.G., J.H. Goodhue, and H.B. Parsell. 1869. *Atlas of Allegany County, New York.* New York: D.G. Beers & Company.

Beers, F.W. 1978. *History of Allegany County, New York 1806–1879.* Ovid: W.E. Morrison & Company.

Benedict, Murray R. 1975. *Farm Policies of the United States 1790–1950.* Millwood NY: Kraus Reprint.

Benson, Lee. 1961. *The Concept of Jacksonian Democracy: New York as a Test Case.* Princeton: Princeton University Press.

———. 1955. *Railroad Regulation and New York Politics.* New York: Russell and Russell.

Benson, Lee, Joel H. Sibley and Phyllis F. Field. 1978. Toward a Theory of Stability and Change in American Voting Patterns: New York State, 1792–1970. In Joel H. Sibley, Allen G. Bogue and William H. Flanigan, eds. *The History of American Electoral Behavior.* Princeton: Princeton University Press.

Berger, Michael L. 1979. *The Devil Wagon in God's Country: The Automobile and Social Change in Rural America 1893–1929.* Hamden CT: Archon Books.

Besser, Terry L. and Margaret M. Hanson. 2004. Development of Last Resort: The Impact of New State Prisons on Small Town Economies in the United States. *Journal of the Community Development Society*, 35:2.

Bolivar Sesquicentennial 1975. Bolivar Free Library.

Bond, M. C. 1947. *Allegany County: Agriculture and Land Use.* Ithaca: Department of Agricultural Economics, Cornell University.

Boris, Emmett and John E. Jeuck. 1950. *Catalogs and Counters: A History of the Sears Roebuck and Company.* Chicago: University of Chicago Press.

Bouton, Terry. 2000. A Road Closed: Rural Insurgency in Post Independence Pennsylvania. *Journal of American History*, 87:3 December.

Bowers, William L. 1974. *The Country Life Movement in America 1900–1920.* Port Washington: Kennikat Press.

Brooks, Charles E. 1996. *Frontier Settlement and Market Revolution: The Holland Land Purchase.* Ithaca: Cornell University Press.

Burnham, Walter Dean. 1981. The System of 1896: An Analysis. In Paul Kleppner et.al., *The Evolution of American Electoral Systems.* Westport CT: Greenwood Press.

Cairncross, Francis. 1997. *The Death of Distance: How the Communications Revolution is Changing our Lives.* Cambridge: Harvard Business School Press.

Carter, Goodrich. 1960. *Government Promotion of American Canals and Railroads 1800–1890.* Westport CT: Greenwood Press.

Chazanoff, William. 1996. Land Speculation in 18th Century New York. In Joseph R. Frese and Jacob Judd, eds. *Business Enterprise in Early New York.* Tarrytown NY: Sleepy Hollow Press.

Cherlin, Andrew. 1996. *Public and Private Families.* New York: McGraw Hill.

Child, Hamilton. 1875. *Gazetteer and Business Directory of Allegany County, NY for 1875.* Syracuse.

Clark, Colin. 1987. Deforestation and Floods. *Environmental Conservation*, 14:1 Spring.

Clifford, Edward Clark. 1986. *The American Family Home 1800–1960.* Chapel Hill: University of North Carolina Press.

Cochrane, Willard W. and Mary P. Ryan. 1976. *American Farm Policy 1948–1973.* Minneapolis: University of Minnesota Press.

Cressey, George B. 1966. Land Forms. In John H. Thompson, ed. *Geography of New York State.* Syracuse: Syracuse University Press.

Cronon, William. 1983. *Changes in the Land: Indians, Colonists and the Ecology of New England.* New York: Hill and Wang.

———. *1991. Nature's Metropolis: Chicago and the Great West.* New York: W. W. Norton & Co.

D'Autremont Family Papers. Angelica Library.

Davis, James E. 1977. *Frontier America 1800–1840.* Glendale CA: Arthur H. Clark.

Denhom, David B. 2006. *Born in the Country: A History of Rural America.* Baltimore: The Johns Hopkins University Press.

Dillon, John J. 1941. *Seven Decades of Milk: A History of New York's Dairy Industry.* New York: Orange Judd Publishing Company.

Directory of Allegany County N Y 1905. Elmira: George Hanford.

Drabenstott, Mark. 2000. Beyond Agriculture: New Policies for Rural America. *Economic Review*, Federal Reserve Bank of Kansas City.

"Dream Home . . . or Nightmare?" 1988. *Consumer Reports*, February.

Easterlin Richard. 1976. Population Change and Farm Settlement in the Northern United States. *Journal of Economic History*, Volume 36.

Ellis, David K. 1969. *The Frontier in American Development.* Ithaca: Cornell University Press.

Ellis, Frost and Fink. 1964. *New York: The Empire State.* New York: Prentice Hall.

Finke, Roger and Rodney Stark. 1992. *The Churching of America: Winners and Losers in our Religious Economy.* Rutgers: Rutgers University Press.

Fitchen, Janet M. 1991. *Endangered Spaces, Enduring Places: Change, Identity and Survival in Rural America.* Boulder: Westview Press.

Flink, James J. 1988. *The Automobile Age.* Cambridge: MIT Press.

Formisano, Ronald P. 1976. Toward a Reorientation of Jacksonian Politics: A Review of the Literature, 1959–1975. *Journal of American History*, Volume 64, June.

Friedberger, Mark. 1988. *Farm Families and Change in Twentieth Century America.* Lexington: University Press of Kentucky.

Gardner, Harry. *Angelica Collecteana.* unpublished manuscript, Angelica Public Library, n.d.

Gates, Paul W. 1960. *The Farmer's Age: Agriculture 1815–1860.* New York: Holt Rinehart Winston.

Gelertner, Mark. 1999. *History of American Architecture.* Hanover: University Press of New England.

Glasmier, Amy K. 1991. *The High Tech Potential: Economic Development in Rural America.* New Brunswick: Rutgers University Press.

Gold Steven D. and Sarah Ritchie. 1994. The Role of the State in the Finances of Cities and Counties in New York. In Jeffrey M. Stonecash, John Kenneth White and Peter W. Colby, eds. *Governing New York State*, 3rd ed. Albany: State University of New York Press.

Gottfried, Herbert, and Jan Jennings. 1988. *American Vernacular Design.* Ames: Iowa State University Press.

Green, John C., Mark J. Rozell and Clyde Wilcox, eds. 2003. *The Christian Right in American Politics.* Washington: Georgetown University Press.

Green, Susan. *A Loom at Every Hearth: Early Intestacy Inventories of Allegany County New York.* unpublished manuscript.

Gunn, L. Ray. 1988. *The Decline of Authority: Public Economic Policy and Political Development in New York, 1800–1860.* Ithaca: Cornell University Press.

Handlin, David P. 1979. *The American Home: Architecture and Society, 1815–1915.* Boston: Little Brown.

Hecht, Michael, ed. 1998. *Communicating Prejudice.* Thousand Oaks, CA: Sage Publications.

Heinrich, Bernd. 1997. *The Trees in My Forest.* New York: Harper Collins.

Herrick, John P. 1952. *Bolivar New York: Pioneer Oil Town.* Los Angeles: The Ward Ritchie Press.

Hill, Ingrid. 1999. "A Poetics of Trailer Park Class." *Peace Review*, June.

History of Tanner Brothers Canning Factory. n.d., Belfast Historical Society.

Humphrey, Thomas J. 2004. *Land and Liberty: Hudson Valley Riots in the Age of Revolution.* DeKalb: Northern Illinois University Press.

Huston, Reeve. 2000. *Land and Freedom: Rural Society, Popular Protest and Party Politics in Antebellum New York.* New York: Oxford University Press.

Israel, Fred L. 1968. *1897 Sears Roebuck Catalog.* Chelsea House Publishers.

Jaffee, David. 1991. Peddlers of Progress and the Transformation of the Rural North. *Journal of American History*, Volume 78, September.

Jakle, John A., Robert W. Bastian and Douglas K. Meyer. 1989. *Common Houses in America's Small Towns: The Atlanta Seaboard to the Mississippi Valley.* Athens: University of Georgia Press.

Jensen, Joan. 1986. *Loosening the Bonds: Mid Atlantic Farm Women 1750–1850.* New Haven: Yale University Press.

Jensen, Richard. 1981. The Last Party System. In Paul Kleppner et.al. *The Evolution of American Electoral Systems.* Westport CT: Greenwood Press.

Johnson, Curtis D. 1989. *Islands of Holiness: Rural Religion in Upstate New York 1790–1860.* Ithaca: Cornell University Press.

Judd, Dennis R. and Todd Swanstrom. 2002. *City Politics.* New York: Longman.

Kass, Alvin. 1965. *Politics in New York State, 1800–1830.* Syracuse: Syracuse University Press.

Kershner, Bruce. 1995. *Ancient Forests of Western New York.* Niagara Falls: Niagara Frontier Botanical Society.

Kilborn, Peter. 2002. Mobile Home Owners Remain House Hungry. *New York Times*, July 11.

Kipp, David L. 1999. *Locking the Heights: The Rise and Demise of the Genesee Valley Canal.*

Kleppner, Paul et. al. 1981. *The Evolution of American Electoral Systems.* Westport, CT: Greenwood Press.

Kriger, Thomas. 1977. Syndicalism and Spilled Milk: The Origins of Dairy Farmer Activism in New York State, 1936–1941. *Labor History*, Volume 38:2, Spring.

Krugman, Paul. 1955. *Development Geography and Economic Theory.* Cambridge: MIT Press.

Lampard, Eric E. 1963. *The Rise of the Dairy Industry in Wisconsin: A Study in Agricultural Change 1820 –1920.* Madison: State Historical Society of Wisconsin.

Latham's Village Directory 1900–1903.

Leahy, Michael and Kurt S. Pregitzer. 2003. A Comparison of Presettlement and Present-day Forests in Northeastern Lower Michigan. *The American Midland Naturalist*, Volume 149:1, January.

Leet, Don R. 1976. The Determinants of the Fertility Transition in Antebellum Ohio. *Journal of Economic History,* Volume 36.

Local New York State Clippings. 1874. Volume 10, Fillmore, Wide Awake Club Library.

Lowry, Ira S. 1966. *Migration and Metropolitan Growth.* San Francisco: Chandler Publishing Company.

Lyson, Thomas A. and William W. Falk. 1993. *Forgotten Places: Uneven Development in Rural America.* Lawrence: University of Kansas Press.

Mark, Irving. 1965. *Agrarian Conflict in Colonial New York 1711–1775.* Port Washington NY: Ira J. Freedman Inc.

Matsch, Charles L. 1976. *North America and the Great Ice Age.* New York: McGraw Hill.

Mau, Clayton. 1944. *The Development of Central and Western New York.* Rochester: Dubois Press.

McCormick, Richard. 1966. *The Second American Party System: Party Formation in the Jacksonian Era.* Chapel Hill: University of North Carolina Press.

McGovern, Mark and Thomas Rasmussen. 2003. *Land Elevation and Early Settlement Patterns in Western New York.* New York State History Conference, Annandale-on-Hudson, June 5, 2003.

McKibben, Bill. 1995. An Explosion of Green. *The Atlantic Monthly*, April.

McMurry, Sally. 1988. *Families and Farmhouses in 19th Century America.* New York: Oxford University Press.

———. 1995. *Transforming Rural Life: Dairying Families and Agricultural Change 1820–1885.* Baltimore: Johns Hopkins University Press.

McNall, Neil. 1952. *An Agricultural History of the Genesee Valley 1790–1860.* Westport: Greenwood Press.

Merrill, Julia Tarbell. 1908. *Rushford Centennial 1808–1908.* Rushford.

Miller, Roberta Balstad. 1979. *City and Hinterland: A Case Study of Urban Growth and Development.* Westport CT: Greenwood Press.

Minard, John. 1896. *Allegany and Its People.* Alfred: W. A. Fergusson.

Mintz, Max. 1999. *Seeds of Empire: The American Revolutionary Conquest of the Iroquois.* New York: New York University Press.

Moon, Dreama G. and Gary L. Rolison. 1998. Communication of Classism, In Michael L. Hecht, ed. *Communicating Prejudice.* Thousand Oaks CA: Sage Publications.

Moore, Abby. The Modern Age. In Jeffrey Howe, ed. 2002. *The Houses We Live In.* London: PRC Publishing Ltd.

Mouth of the Creek: The History of Fillmore New York. Fillmore.

Neth, Mary. 1995. *Preserving the Family Farm.* Baltimore: The Johns Hopkins University Press.

Newman, Monroe. 1972. *The Political Economy of Appalachia.* Lexington MA: D. C. Heath & Co.

New York Agricultural Statistics Service. 2000. *Allegany County Farm Statistics.* Albany: *www.nass.usda.gov/ny.*

Norden, D. Sven. 1974. *Rich Harvest: A History of the Grange, 1867–1900.* Jackson: University of Mississippi.

North, Douglas. 1966. *The Economic Growth of the United States 1790–1960.* New York: W. W. Norton.

O'Hare William and Barbara O'Hare. 1993. Upward Mobility. *American Demographics*, January.

Oliver, Chadwick, and Bruce Larson. 1996. *Forest Stand Dynamics.* New York: John Wiley.

Olson, Mancur. 1965. *The Logic of Collective Action.* Cambridge: Harvard University Press.

Ordeshook, Peter C. 1986. *Game Theory and Political Theory: An Introduction.* New York: Cambridge University Press.

Osterud, Nancy Grey. 1991. *Bonds of Community: The Lives of Farm Women in Nineteenth Century New York.* Ithaca: Cornell University Press.

Parkerson, Donald H. 1995. *The Agricultural Transition in New York State: Markets and Migration in Mid-Nineteenth Century America.* Ames: Iowa State University Press.

Patterson, Russell. 1998. *Estimating Tourism Impacts of Deer Hunting in New York State: A Case Study of 1997 Deer Take Data.* unpublished manuscript.

Peterson, Fred W. 1992. *Homes in the Heartland: Balloon Frame Farm Houses of the Upper Middle West, 1850–1920.* Lawrence: University of Kansas Press.

Peterson, Thomas. 2001. *Linked Arms: A Rural Community Resists Nuclear Waste.* Albany: State University of New York Press.

Petri, Pitt. 1960. *The Postal History of Western New York.* unpublished ms, Allegany County Historical Society.

Pierce, Harry H. 1953. *Railroads of New York: A Study of Government Aid 1826–1875.* Cambridge: Harvard University Press.

Potter, Clifford M. 1968. *Cheese Factories of Allegany County.* Alfred: Alfred Historical Society.

Primack, Martin. 1962. Land Clearing Under 19th Century Techniques. *Journal of Economic History*, Volume 22.

Rae, John B. 1965. *The American Automobile.* Chicago: University of Chicago Press.

Rasmussen, Thomas H. 1990. Landfill Development in Rural New York? *Empire State Report*, Volume 16, July.

———. 2001. Transportation Costs, Economies of Scale and Early Settlement Patterns in Western New York. *Pioneer America Society Transactions*, Volume 24.

Reynolds, John F. 1962. *The Almond Story: The Early Years.* Hornell: John F. Reynolds.

Richardson, Harry W. 1973. *Regional Growth Theory.* New York: Macmillan.

Richter, Daniel K. 1992. *Ordeal of the Longhouse: The Peoples of the Iroquois League in the Era of European Colonization.* Chapel Hill: University of North Carolina Press.

Ryan, Mary P. 1981. *Cradle of the Middle Class: The Family in Oneida County New York, 1790–1865.* New York: Cambridge University Press.

——. 1975. *Womanhood in America: From Colonial Times to the Present*. New York: Harper and Row.

Scharff, Virginia. 1991. *Taking the Wheel: Women and the Coming of the Motor Age*. New York: The Free Press.

Scully, Vincent J. Jr. 1971. *The Shingle Style and the Stick Style*. New Haven: Yale University Press.

Sellers, Charles. 1991. *The Market Revolution: Jacksonian America, 1815–1846*. New York: Oxford University Press.

Shaw, R. Paul. 1975. *Migration Theory and Fact*. Philadelphia: Regional Science Research Institute.

Sibley, Robert W. 1969. Frontier Attitudes and Debt Collection in Western New York. In David K. Ellis. *The Frontier in American Development*. Ithaca: Cornell University Press.

Slade, William G. 1981. Political Pluralism and Party Development: The Creation of a Modern Party System: 1815–1852. In Paul Kleppner et al. *The Evolution of American Electoral Systems*. Westport CT: Greenwood Press.

Small, Nora Pat. 1997. New England Farm Houses in the Early Republic: Rhetoric and Reality. In Carter L. Hudgins and Elizabeth Collins Cromley, eds. *Shaping Communities: Perspectives in Vernacular Architecture*. Knoxville: University of Tennessee Press.

Smith, Marion J. 1895. *History of Fillmore*.

Spafford, Horatio Gates. 1981. *A Gazetteer of the State of New York, 1824*. Interlaken: Heart of the Lakes Publishing.

Stamm, Eugene R. 1991. *The History of Cheese Making in New York State*. Endicott NY: Lewis Group.

Stommel, Henry and Elizabeth Stommel, 1979. The Year Without a Summer. *Scientific American*, Volume 240, June.

Summerhill, Thomas 2005. *Harvest of Dissent: Agrarianism in Nineteenth Century New York*. Urbana: University of Illinois Press.

Sundquist, James L. 1983. *Dynamics of the Party System: Alignment and Realignment of Political Parties in the United States*, Washington: Brookings Institution.

Taylor, George Rogers. 1951. *The Transportation Revolution 1815–1860*, Armonk: M.E. Sharpe.

Temin, Peter. 1966. Steam and Waterpower in the Early 19th Century. *Journal of Economic History*, Volume 26.

Tryon, Robert Milton. 1917. *Household Manufactures in the United States 1640–1860*. Chicago: Chicago University Press.

Wallace, Anthony F.C. 1970. *The Death and Rebirth of the Seneca*. New York. Alfred A. Knopf.

Wallace, Anthony F. C. 1978. *Rockdale: The Growth of an American Village in the Early Industrial Revolution*. New York: Alfred A. Knopf.

Wallace, Michael. 1968. Changing Concepts of Party in the United States: New York 1815–1828. *American History Review*, December.

Weil, Gordon L. 1977. *Sears Roebuck USA: The Great American Catalog Store*. New York: Stein and Day.

Wessels, Tom. 1977. *Reading the Forested Landscape.* Woodstock VT: The Country-man Press.

White, P.L. 1979. *Beekmantown New York: Forest Frontier to Farm Community.* Austin: University of Texas Press.

Whitney Gordon G. 1994. *From Coastal Wilderness to Fruited Plain.* Cambridge: Cambridge University Press.

Williams, John Alexander. 2002. *Appalachia: A History.* Chapel Hill: University of North Carolina Press.

Williams, Michael. 1989. *Americans & Their Forests.* Cambridge: Cambridge University Press.

Woodruff, John. 1942. *Geology of the Wellsville, Quadrangle New York.* Albany: New York State Museum Bulletin.

Wyckoff, William. 1981. Assessing Land Quality in Western New York: The Township Surveys of 1797–1799. *Surveying and Mapping* Volume 41:3.

Winter, Robert. 1995. *American Bungalow Style.* New York: Simon and Schuster.

Wright, Gwendolyn. 1981. *Building the Dream: A Social History of Housing in America.* New York: Pantheon Books.

Zipf, George K. 1949. *Human Behavior and the Principle of Least Effort.* Cambridge: Addison Wesley Press.

Index

agriculture: clearing the land, 44–50; declining farm production after WWII, 150–53; farm ownership and inheritance, 83, 150–53; low farm productivity on the frontier, 48; promise of agricultural life, 93–95; quality of rural life in 20th century, 126–29; rising land prices and higher productivity, 52, 69; Rushford and Willing 1875 and 1905, 102–5; social consequences of cash crop farming, 72–74, 126–27; subsistence to cash crop farming, 68–74; technological innovations, 71
Alfred, 18, 20, 23, 80
Allegany River, 16–19
Allen, 81–85
Almond, 28, 30, 80, 87–91, 133
Alma, 68, 70, 91–93, 151
Amish farmers, 151
Amity, 20, 24, 71, 87–91, 133
Andover, 68
Angelica, 3, 18, 30, 64, 71, 115
automobile: impact of Ford's Model T, 138–41; suburbanization, 157–58

Belfast, 29, 68, 70, 87–91
Belmont, 68, 94

Birdsall, 71, 91–93, 133
Bolivar, 20, 22, 24, 133, 151

churches. *See* religion
Caneadea, 18, 36, 68, 71, 133
central place, 1, 3, 28
Centerville, 18, 20, 26, 29, 81–85
Ceres, 63
cheese making. *See* dairy
Church, Philip, 30, 38–39, 64
Civil War: effect on price of labor, 92; origins of Republican Party, 95
Clarksville, 68, 91–93, 151
commercial activity in villages: decline, Main Street Wellsville after WWII, 148–50; Main Street shops, 1875 and 1905, 105–9; Sears and Montgomery Ward catalogs, 110–11
community values: effect of cash cropping on ties with neighbors, 69, 72–73; links with neighbors on the frontier, 57–58; mistrust of strangers, 55–56, 114–15; role of women in maintaining, 111–13
country life movement, 127–28
creditors and debtors, 37–44
Cuba, 20, 25, 63, 87–91

dairy farming: beginnings before the railroad, 52; cheese factories, numbers and size, 131; cheese making, 99–100; decline of dairy after 1900, 129–30; early and late adoption by town, 69; elevation and farm abandonment, 20th century, 132–33; expansion of dairy farming, 99–102; future of dairy farm, 150–53; women in dairy production, 73–74, 152

Dairyman's league, Dairy Farmer's Union, 130–31

D'Autremont family: Alexandre's difficult wife, 55; mistrust of Native Americans in 1812, 35; standard of living on the frontier, 47, 50

deer, 51, 177

Democratic Party, 58–61, 124–25, 136–37, 164

demographic transition, 82–83

Douglas, Frederick, 78, 96–97

Dupont, Victor and Josephine, 21, 55, 66

Dyke, Nathaniel, 30

early settlement patterns, 15; closeness to market towns, 2, 22–27; elevation and, 2, 22–27; importance of neighbors, 3, 16–19

economic trends: agriculture, commerce and industry in 1865 and 2000, 146–47; centers of growth and economic backwaters in 1855, 86–93; measures of social well being, 2000, 155–56

economies of scale, 3, 128, 145, 178

Ellicott, Joseph, 40, 179

Erie Canal, 19, 21, 29, 70

Erie Railroad, 2, 70, 80

Fillmore, 57, 105–7, 127, 139

free rider problem, 7, 130

Friendship, 3, 18, 133, 156

game theory, 5

Genesee, 68, 91–93, 151

Genesee River, 16–19, 24, 29

Genesee Valley Canal, 2, 70, 80

Geographic Information Systems (GIS), 22

Grange, 112–13

Granger, 29, 81–85, 133

Grove, 20, 26, 29, 91–93

Holland Land Company, 40, 43, 48

housing styles: automobile, impact of, 157–63; balloon frame construction, 82; bungalow style, 141–42; Federalist, 62–63; Gothic revival, 66–67; Greek Revival, 65; housing stock by date of construction, 143–44; inhabitants of typical farm house, 1855, 82; interior space, organization of, 76, 117, 141–42; Italianate and Italian Villa, 75–76; log and sawn lumber material, 81; manufactured housing, 158–63; Queen Anne (Victorian), 94, 117–19, 141; ranch, 157–58

industry: decline after WWII, 146–47; petroleum, 123–24, 178; processing grain, hides and lumber, 1840–1865, 76–79; in Rushford and Willing, 1905, 105–9; Tanner Brothers factory, 120–21

Iroquois, 34–36

Karr Valley, 30, 40, 133–35

landlords and tenants, 38

land prices, 40, 86, 102

land ownership and inheritance, 83–84

landscape, changes, 13–15, 171–77

low level radioactive waste, 169–71

lumbering: as attack on nature, 45–46; clearing the land, 47–48; decline, 68, 101; sawmills, 30; Susquehanna

River valley, 19, 29; uses of wood on frontier, 49–50

manufactured housing, 158–63
maple sugar production, 50
migration, 16, 83, 45–46
mobile home. *See* manufactured housing

native Americans. *See* Iroquois
New Hudson, 70

petroleum industry, 123–24, 178
Phelps and Gorham Land Company, 37
Pittsburgh, Shawmut and Northern Railroad, 71
politics: Bryan, William Jennings and election of 1896, 137; before 1828, 58; county taxing and spending trends, 166–68; declining influence of western New York, 164; economic interests and moral values, 137, 164; New York State mandates, 166–68; post civil war, 124–26; Republicans and Democrats, 95–97, 124–26, 136–37, 164; Roosevelt's New Deal, 137; town governments, 179–80; waste disposal issues, 169–71; Whigs and Democrats, 58–61; women's suffrage, 136
population: demographic transition, 82–83; population growth and decline, 68; population, 1820–1850, 16–18; population in 2000, 153–55
potash, 49
Prisoner's dilemma, 6; creditors and debtors, 37–44; farmers and shopkeepers, 72–73; farmers withholding milk from market, 130–31; farm women and hired help, 127; games among neighbors, 53–54; husbands and wives, 54–55; landlords and tenants, 38; native Americans and early settlers, 36; settlers and strangers, 55–56, 114

railroads: discriminatory pricing, 100–101; local investments in, 71
religion, 57
Republican Party, 95–98, 164, 136–37
rural life, quality of , 126–29
Rushford, 44, 87–91, 102–5

sawmills: construction, 30; core local industry in 1840, 76–77; deforestation and flooding, 79; economic importance, 78–79
school consolidation, 128–29
Seneca Indians. *See* Iroquois
Seventh Day Baptists, 46
sheep raising, 52
Sinclair Oil Company, 123
specialization as economic principle, 3–5, 178
standard of living: on the frontier, 50–51; post civil war prosperity, 99–109; post WWII, 146–50
Susquehanna River, 9, 19–20, 23, 29, 80

Tanner Brothers canning factory, 120–21
textile manufacturing, 52
trailer. *See* manufactured homes
transportation costs: demise of railroad, 148–50; discriminatory railroad pricing, 100–101; early road building, 30–32; effect on human settlement patterns, 11, 20; impact of railroad and canal, 69; automobile and, 138–45; interstate highway system, 179; Turnpike Road construction, 30–32
Troup, Robert S., 43
Turnpike Road, 30–32, 41, 133–34

villages as central places, 28–30, 74–75

War of 1812: alliance, England and Iroquois, 34–36; impact on early settlement patterns, 16

watersheds and early settlement patterns, 22–27
Wellsville, 68, 87–91, 105–9, 148–50
wheat growing, 30
Whigs, 58–61
Whitesville, 3
Williamson, Charles, 37–38
Willing, 102–5
Women: defending moral values, 112–14; in the work force, 119–20; managing the home, 116–17; numbers of men and women, 92, 141; players in household games, 54; role in dairy production, 73–74; social status in patriarchal culture, 54–55; suffrage movement,136; use of automobile, 139
wool manufacture, 55
Wright, Frank Lloyd, 157

About the Author

Thomas Rasmussen has spent many hours hiking the Finger Lakes Trail with his wife Margaret, spotting the plants, stone fences and foundations of early farmsteads and has walked the streets of Allegany County villages in search of how houses and communities have evolved over time.

He is emeritus Professor of Political Science and Environmental Studies at Alfred University where he taught for 35 years. He has coauthored books on *American Government and State and Local Politics* and written numerous journal articles on environmental policy. He has delivered papers on Western New York domestic architecture, the changing dairy industry and the evolution of the Allegany County landscape from forest to pasture and back to forest.